SUCCESS WITHOUT COLLEGE

Careers in the Law

DATE DUE		

SUCCESS WITHOUT COLLEGE

Careers in the Law

By Tracy A. Cinocca, J.D./ M.B.A.

BARRON'S

All inquiries should be addressed to:
Barron's Educational Series, Inc.
250 Wireless Boulevard
Hauppauge, New York 11788
http://www.barronseduc.com

Library of Congress Catalog Card No. 2001018498

International Standard Book No. 0-7641-1654-1

Library of Congress Cataloging-in-Publication Data

Cinocca, Tracy A.
    Careers in the law / by Tracy A. Cinocca.
        p.   cm.—(Success without college series)
    Includes bibliographical references and index.
    ISBN 0-7641-1654-1
    1. Practice of law—Vocational guidance—United States.   2. Justice,
Administration of—Vocational guidance—United States.   I. Title.
II. Success without college.
KF297 .C56 2001
340'.023'73—dc21
                                                                    2001018498

Printed in Hong Kong

9   8   7   6   5   4   3   2   1

Contents

CONTENTS

Careers in the Law

Careers in the Law addresses prospective legal employment fields, including secretaries, legal assistants, legal administrators, legal marketers, political consultants, court reporters, private investigators, deputy court clerks, and mediators, as well as other legal support personnel. Also included is practical information on expectations of a legal career and how to develop it, along with résumé writing and interview tips. Comprehensive Internet resources and professional connections are included as well.

How to Use This Book

As an aspiring or current legal professional, you should read this entire book so you can become familiar with your career options and transition to a new legal career. Many of the careers in this book have responsibilities that overlap other careers. By being familiar with all careers in the legal field, you will be able to more effectively direct your legal career path and make appropriate employment decisions. The legal profession is a highly competitive one for which you should plan as early as possible. Through an investigation of career options in the legal field without a law degree, and all the qualifications, training, experience, and certifications you can amass, you can prepare for excellence in your chosen profession.

Acknowledgments

A number of colleagues, friends, family and legal professionals have contributed to the quality of this manuscript, among them: Kelly Bryant, Bryant Court Reporting; Jean Benzel, Legal Secretary; Gary Moore, Private Investigator, Accurate Investigations; Annetta Smith, Legal Assistant; Jeanne Day, Legal Administrator; Gary Weitzel, Administrator, Information and Membership Resources Association of Legal Administrators; Joe Valencia, Bail Agent with Josh Herman; Rick Carpenter, Political Consultant; Mozghan Mizban, Director of Client Services at Cooley Godward LLP; Joseph Paulk, President of Dispute Resolution Consultants; John Kloiber, Jr., Mediator; Sally Howe-Smith, Tulsa County Court Clerk; Aimee Walker, Temporary Employee; Kathryn W. Cinocca, my mom; Sue Tate, Oklahoma ADR Director; Ann Wilkins, Early Settlement Northeast Mediation Director; Norman Fujioka, Program Manager, Volunteers in Public Service to the Courts Program, Hawaii; Chad A. Fleming; Max Reed, my editor; and my son Javen C. Cinocca.

This book is dedicated with love to my mother, son, and best friend.

CHAPTER ONE

Career Expectations in Law

Those in search of occupational excitement and drama should consider a career in law. Television networks enhance a glamorous stereotype of the legal profession in such programs as *Law and Order*, *Family Law*, and *The Practice*. However, television networks—and movie production companies as well—take this perception to extremes in such sitcoms as *Ally McBeal* and *Ed*, and such movies as *The Firm*. These same productions stress the high work ethic and commitment required for the dedicated professionals portrayed. The intermittent excitement and drama of a legal career should be weighed against the toll of intellectual competitiveness, emotional strain, and rigorous work schedule. If the toll is acceptable to you, then you may enjoy a legal career path more than any other field.

As an aspiring legal professional, you should have some idea about what to expect from a legal career. Each chapter in this book specifically addresses what you may expect in each career discussed. However, there are other expectations that permeate most legal careers and vary depending upon employers. The objective is to know what will be expected of you professionally and what you may expect personally. Also, you should have certain expectations of the legal field as a whole and be wary enough to avoid unhealthy or unpleasant work environments.

IN THE BEGINNING

People who work in legal careers evolve intellectually and emotionally. At the beginning of your career, you will likely spin your wheels on many unproductive tangents, and suffer anxiety as you attempt to properly complete your tasks, but your confidence will increase along with your competence and efficiency, while your anxiety decreases. During this process your training and experience will promote objectivity without the emotion commonly created by the excitement and drama of your new career. However, there will always be some degree of excitement and drama no matter how entrenched in the legal mind-set you become. Initially, you will probably not be able to enjoy the drama very much, and you will react to it due to a lack of experience. Later, your experiences will prevent the excitement and drama from taking hold of you and allow you to enjoy your career and the opportunities created by it to help others. Patience and perseverance through the rigors of learning your new trade will pay off.

PERSONAL TRANSFORMATION

The personal relationships of most legal professionals may change when they grow with the experience and wisdom that a legal career accelerates through training and the implementation of legal analysis. First, as a legal professional you should expect to constantly face self-evaluation of morals and beliefs when you hear different factual scenarios and are forced to apply a systematic evaluation of results. For example, when a disabled mother has been the primary caregiver of a child and the father has been absent due to work or school, who should receive primary custody? What is in the child's best interest? The answer requires a systematic approach to the case, especially with regard to specific facts applied to the law. Your analysis may be influenced by your personal values about disabled people, primary caregivers, whether or not children should remain with their mothers, and absent fathers. You should need more facts to complete this analysis and form your opinions, although you probably already have a few opinions based on these facts. Legal professionals develop their sense of justice and equity when they use a mature and rational approach to sensitive issues, while, hopefully, maintaining compassion, tempered with professionalism and integrity.

LEGAL ANALYSIS

Legal analysis demands objectivity and resistance to emotional interference, even if the values are at odds with the results of legal analysis. Legal professionals learn how to exercise sound judgment based on facts in their professional and personal lives, thereby increasing their interpersonal communication skills. They should expect that the law involves a lower standard of care than morality. This means that legal analysis does not always provide an assessment of what is morally right, equitable, or just. As the saying goes, you can't legislate morality or common sense into people. Legal analysis merely provides an assessment of strengths and weaknesses of a person's position as applied to the law. It is a legal professional's job to apply the law and not necessarily morality, unless it is expedient to do so in conjunction with arguments. Laypeople are consistently frustrated with results; justice may not always appear to be served. Further, just because some legal professionals may adhere to a lower standard of care than they should does not mean you should do the same. However, you can expect frustration or rewards due to inconsistent results between the law and morality depending upon what side of the case you are on. For example, if your firm has a client you know is guilty of some heinous crime, but there was an illegal search and your efforts help to acquit the accused, you will likely be rewarded for your efforts even though the result may be contrary to morality. You may also be faced with a situation where judgment or sentence was imposed on someone inequitably. These situations may be hard pills to swallow.

CHECKING THE FACTS ABOUT CLIENTS

Legal professionals should expect to develop an ability to determine whether or not others are credible, and double-check the facts. When legal professionals rely on the representation of a client, an employer, or an adverse party, they may suffer negative consequences if that representation is not true. Such misplaced reliance impairs the integrity of legal professionals and could cost them their jobs. For example, pretend your firm's client claims that an adverse party shaved his head before a hair analysis in order to frustrate a likely positive drug test result. You then provide that information to an attorney who argues the point in court. The adverse party brings photographs to court that show the client had little or no hair for a year prior to the drug test. In retrospect, the firm's client explains this by saying it had always been at least an inch longer on the top. At this point, the credibility of the client comes into question, and the firm's efforts are impaired. You should always acquire the most detailed statement of facts possible, and double-check the facts.

CHECKING THE FACTS ABOUT EMPLOYERS

Legal professionals should check facts that matter with employers or get them in writing. Let's say that an employer represents to you in your job interview that you will receive a raise within three months to a year, and likely within three months, if you work hard. There is no written contract stating this—you rely on this representation, work hard with excellent performance, yet are refused a raise after six months. Then, coincidentally, after one year, you receive your first negative performance evaluation. Obviously, your loyalty and dedication to this employer were misplaced; your employer did not keep his promise. Also, had you talked to others employed by this fictional firm before accepting the job offer, you may have learned that no one *ever* received a raise in the time they worked there. This would have let you know that it was highly unlikely that the employer ever intended to keep its promise of a raise; had you further investigated the employer and its representations, you would have saved yourself the disappointment and grief caused by the misrepresentation. With more realistic expectations of the veracity of others, you would not have relied on it.

CHECKING THE FACTS FROM OTHER LEGAL PROFESSIONALS

Pretend a legal professional represents a parent corporation that does not have at least 15 employees as required under statute to sue them. When you visit the parent corporation's web site, it is listed with an excess of 100,000 employees. Had you relied exclusively on this representation, your firm's client would have lost the opportunity to become an indispensable party to a suit. Legal professionals learn to assess others' credibility, reliability, and knowledge, without excuse or self-doubt. They learn how to prevent misplaced loyalty and trust from impairing their integrity, affecting their personal lives, or harming a client's case. To some extent, legal professionals lower their expectations of others; in other words, they take whatever is said with a grain of salt. Just because someone says something that is untrue or misleading does not necessarily mean they intentionally misrepresented the facts. Newfound abilities in your career should spill over into your personal life, thereby enhancing your interpersonal and communication skills and increasing your confidence and conviction of beliefs.

FIRMS' AND ORGANIZATIONAL ENVIRONMENTS

As in any other profession, legal professionals may expect to encounter employers that foster secretive or territorial environments. Every law firm has its own character and philosophy. Although most attorneys are honest and professional, there are those that prompt numerous derogatory jokes about the profession, comparing attorneys to a variety of cold-blooded creatures. Remember: The legal profession is an adversarial one and generally a win/lose situation. However, legal professionals should avoid becoming entangled with any firms or organizations that may arouse suspicion that the jokes are well founded. Legal professionals should feel that they fit into an office situation with their integrity intact.

A well-established base of principles upon which to assess employers and govern responses will help you select the right employer, and leave if an employer is not right. Expect to take constructive criticism without argument and deference, especially when learning a new trade. After one year at a firm or organization, as a legal professional you should feel more confident with increased self-respect in your position. If not, you should seek a more appropriate employment match. Becoming a legal professional is an investment that will strengthen your character, resolve, and tenacity.

SALARIES

Starting salaries are higher for entry-level legal professionals than for any other profession that is available without a college degree. Many experienced legal personnel can earn substantial incomes after four years' experience, and after five years' experience, legal professionals can probably gross more than many new attorneys and college graduates, without the educational debt. Many legal professionals can generate very high incomes if they have the know-how and courage to start their own businesses.

CODE OF CONDUCT

Clients hire law firms to protect themselves from others. Attorneys are bound by their own code, which details professional responsibility as sentinels and officers of the judicial system. This code protects the public, instills confidence in the judicial system, and maintains the integrity of the judiciary. All legal professionals should adhere to the code as well as to any other code of conduct applicable to their profession, and expect their employers and employees to do so as well. The legal field embraces those legal professionals who wish to bring honor to the profession. Ethical and honest legal professionals enhance the public's perception of the judiciary and attorneys. Unfortunately, as in most professions, the bad apples tend to receive more publicity than the good ones. Legal professionals can bring honor to the profession by following the code of conduct for attorneys and acting according to a higher moral standard than the law is able to mandate.

PROFESSIONAL EXPECTATIONS

Professionally, you may expect that your performance will be constantly scrutinized by attorneys, clients, fellow staff members, and others. Every day, your performance will be reevaluated and assessed. This means that the work product is expected to be letter-perfect before you submit it to supervisors or others. Letter-perfect work product is the result, in part, of following directions, good organization, and thorough review of documents—a lost or missed piece of paper can cost you your job. You should have either a competitive mind-set or be able to deal effectively with competitive people. To constantly measure up to performance standards, you should work hard, avoid gossip, concentrate on multiple paper-intensive tasks, prioritize and manage work loads to reduce stress, and communicate effectively. Through the constant scrutiny legal professionals endure, you may expect your intellectual capabilities to increase, communication skills to improve, and your focus on problem resolution to narrow. These improved abilities will lead to an increase in self-esteem and confidence along with enhanced cognitive abilities.

Overall, you may expect a legal career to provide you with the opportunities to help people in crisis situations; meet many intelligent, eccentric, or fascinating people; increase cognitive abilities; and develop tenacity, resolve, and integrity. But be aware that you should expect to hurdle the obstacles in front of these growth opportunities.

A FEW KEY POINTS TO REMEMBER

- Learn how to control your emotions and maintain professionalism and integrity.
- Be prepared to handle stress from heavy work loads and difficult people by developing nerves of steel, patience, perseverance, diligence, organization, and effective conflict resolution and communication skills.
- Prepare yourself intellectually and mentally as thoroughly as possible for your career in law.
- Adhere to the attorney's code of professional responsibility and that of your particular professional area.
- Legal professionals, on the average, earn more than other professionals who work without a college degree.

CHAPTER TWO

Develop Realistic Expectations

Being told what to expect in a legal career is not as helpful as experiencing it for yourself. There are many ways you can become introduced to the rigors of the legal profession without necessarily making a career commitment. The best way to develop your own expectations is to take the advice in the previous chapter and throughout this text and temper it with actual experience, if you do not already have any. You can develop your own realistic expectations by gaining experience in the law or entering the legal profession through extracurricular activities, courses, internships, temporary work, volunteer activities, and prior employment.

CURRICULUM COURSES

If you are interested in preparing for a legal professional career, you can develop the skills and qualifications early on in order to be a success. If you are already a high school graduate and investigating alternative careers, additional or former education in legal fields is a real plus. Knowing a little bit about everything will be helpful in your career in law, and an education cannot be overlooked.

Aspiring legal professionals should take any vocational or high school courses offered in the field of law. This will show potential employers an early interest to work in a career in law. Specialization or additional courses in the academic fields of English, literature, journalism, foreign languages, and even persuasion in some schools, will help you as an aspiring legal professional to obtain a solid foundation of skills. If you speak a foreign language you may have an advantage over other job applicants at firms or organizations that have a multilingual client base. Further, computer skills courses such as keyboarding, typing, Word, and WordPerfect, along with spreadsheet software such as Lotus and Excel will often help you get your foot in the door at a new firm or organization.

DEBATE CLASSES

By learning litigation tactics in debate class, you will be able to anticipate the needs of attorneys and learn how to research an issue and argue it. Debate principles and procedures apply to oral advocacy, research investigation, and writing briefs. For example, useful debate talents include analyzing evidence; impacting arguments by stating why, how or when; defining words; expressing values only if relevant to claim evaluation; focusing on resolution, instead of generic ideas or values; formulating, comparing, and rebutting arguments; and the obligation to clash with another's views. Debaters learn basic principles inherent in litigation, including discouraged legal tactics that encompass intimidation; incivility; making politically incorrect arguments; saying your opponent agreed to, dropped, or conceded something he or she did not; making new arguments or improperly extending them in rebuttals; and making arguments you said you would not. Debaters manage legal-like stress and anxiety that attorneys and other legal professionals face. This experience can increase your job performance as a legal professional in a support role to an attorney, and mentally prepare you for the rigors of a legal profession.

PUBLIC SPEAKING AND DRAMA CLASSES

Meeting with attorneys, judges, and other law professionals may be intimidating; public speaking and drama can help you learn proper presentation and decorum, even if you are terrified. You should learn to hide your emotion and present a professional demeanor at all times, even if this means an Emmy nomination for your performance. In public speaking class, you will learn how to formulate logical and coherent presentations. In drama class, you will learn how to appeal to audiences, using proper inflection and demeanor.

EXTRACURRICULAR ACTIVITIES

Extracurricular activities can teach legal strategy, negotiation, public speaking, and persuasion, along with political processes. Student government orients people to the legislative branch. The more power vested in a student government association, the more the participants will learn. Some members of student government associations learn how to draft resolutions and bills. Members who do so learn basic principles of drafting pleadings and interpreting laws. In student government, members negotiate and develop supporting factions in the student's interest, in much the same way that legal professionals serve and protect the interests of their clients. Legal analysis can sometimes rest on legislative intent, so, knowing how this process works can help legal professionals conduct better research and present legislative intent behind statutes in order to persuade courts to rule in their client's favor.

INTERNSHIPS

Internships are opportunities to work for a firm or organization in order to acquire experience. Many interns receive little or no pay, but they may receive educational credit from their schools, if allowed. If you have no experience or qualifications and cannot find employment, you could offer to intern for a firm or organization in order to acquire the experience you need and assess the merits of a related career. If you are acquiring an education at a university, high school, or vocational school, you should contact your school to learn whether it offers credits for internships in lieu of other educational requirements.

Legislative internships provide students with an understanding of political and legislative processes. Every internship offers different responsibilities and opportunities for growth and training. Legislative interns may learn about legal, market, and constituency research and how to use the results of such research. They witness firsthand a legislator's personal and professional concerns and how the legislative process operates. Washington, D.C. is the ideal location for a legislative internship. Alternatively, a state internship would expose legal professionals to local politics and provide them with valuable community contacts. An experience as an intern will provide you with invaluable exposure to politics and the law. A legislative internship is directly relevant to a career as a political consultant. Other internships may be available in marketing or management. To investigate whether internships may be appropriate for you, check with your school, local legislators, the relevant chapters in this text, and the following web sites.

InternshipPrograms.com	*http://www.internshipprograms.com/*
InternShip.Com	*http://www.internship.com/*
Internships with the Federal Government	*http://enrollment.csusb.edu/~waiv/intern.html*

Most commonly, internships are readily available for legal assistants, aspiring political consultants, and legal marketing prrofessionals.

TEMPORARY WORK

If you are not sure if you want a career in law, and you need a paycheck, you should explore temporary legal staffing. According to Ameii L. Walker, a long-term temporary employee, "The temporary employment industry is the largest single employer of people in the work force." She likes being a temporary employee for the following reasons.

- She can choose which assignments to accept. Her temporary agency takes care of her when the assignment is not what she expected.

- She can work short-term or long-term assignments and choose to work close to home.

- She is not tied down to one desk, but if she likes the company and they want to hire her, she can accept full-time employment.

Walker says that a lack of benefits and leaving new friends are the biggest pitfalls of temporary work. Her recommendation is that temporary employees take advantage of any and all training classes offered. For more information, and career site links, visit her web site at *http://www.dataoptions.com/temp.html*. Here are some other Internet sites that may be of interest.

ContractJobs.com	*http://www.contract-jobs.com*
Interim Services, Inc.	*http://www.interim.com*
Kelly Services	*http:/www.kellyservices.com*
Manpower	*http://manpower.com*
Net Temps	*http://www.net-temps.com*
Staffing Services	*http://www.staffingservices.com*
Temping.com	*http://www.temping.com*
Temporary Labor Jobs	*http://laborready.com*
Worldwide Freelance Directory	*http://www.cvp.com/freelance*

VOLUNTEER ACTIVITIES

Every state has its own agencies and organizations that need volunteers in the legal community. States generally have programs that accept volunteers to help with domestic violence intervention programs and services, witness protection, district attorney office functions, public defender office functions, indigent defense organizations, mediation, politics and campaigning, legislative assistance, and even tribal courts. More can be learned about national volunteer opportunities that may relate to a legal career at the following web sites.

Action Without Borders	*http://www.idealist.org*
American Red Cross	*http://www.redcross.org.volunteer/vol.html*
ImpactOnline	*http://www.impactonline.org*
Nonprofit Career Network	*http://www.nonprofitcareer.com*
Peace Corps	*http://www.peacecorps.gov/home.html*
Points of Light Foundation	*http://www.pointsoflight.org*
United Nations Volunteers	*http://www.unv.org*
Volunteer Activism Via the Internet	*http://www.serviceleader.org/vv/activist.html*
Volunteer Connections	*http://www.volunteerconnections.org/ vcp_volunteercentermap.cfm*

As a volunteer, you should act with the same level of professionalism and reliability you would as if receiving a salary. This will motivate others to train you and help you learn what you need to know from the experience. The volunteer organizations should expect this of you and treat you accordingly.

PRIOR EMPLOYMENT

Prior employment, even in a non-law-related career, provides legal professionals with greater maturity to handle the rigors of legal employment. By having experience or training in a trade, you can claim that you are particularly suited for any related legal field. Here is a sample of not necessarily law-related trades that, for the most part, can be learned at a vocational school and that could benefit you in your legal career.

Health Care Law, Medical Malpractice, Personal Injury and Insurance Defense

Medical Assisting
Medical Transcription
Biological Technology
Emergency Medical Technician—Paramedic
Health Information Technology—Medical Records
Nursing

Communications and Telecommunications Law/Litigation Skills and Exhibits

Radio/Television Broadcasting
Visual Communication Technology: Graphic Arts/Printing
Visual Communication Technology: Photography–Television

General Law and Skills of Use around a Law Office

Computer Information Technology
Office Technology/Secretarial Science–Clerk Typist
Office Technology/Secretarial Science–Executive
Office Technology/Secretarial Science–Legal
Accounting
Marketing
Administration
Management
Employee Benefits and Payroll

Juvenile Justice and Family Law

Early Childhood Development
Therapists and Counselors

Business/Civil Litigation°

Computer Information Technology
Accounting
Air Conditioning Technology: Heating and Ventilation
Automotive/Mechanical Training
Biological Technology
Business Financial Services
Fashion Buying and Merchandising
Small Business Management
Tooling and Machining
Construction and Carpentry
Civil Technology: Plane Surveying
Manufacturing Technological–Robotics/Automation
Construction and Carpentry

° Practically any job skill in the business community can be made applicable to this area of the law, which is probably the widest in scope.

Criminal Law

Criminal Justice: Corrections Administration
Criminal Justice: Police
Law Enforcement

Law Office Management°

Human Services
Food Industry Management
Food Service Administration
Marketing
Interior Design
Small Business Management
Retail Business Management

° Any experience or training in management will help you manage staff and other attorneys and be considered an asset to any firm.

Environmental Law and Intellectual Property

Electrical Engineering Technology
Electro-Optics Technology
Fire Protection Technology
Heating, Ventilating, Air Conditioning
Hotel Technology
Industrial Instrumentation Technology
Mechanical Technology
Chemical Technology
Civil Technology
Construction Technology

International Law

International Business

At the very least, experience or training in a trade will provide you with better comprehension of the business concerns and customs in your community, as encountered by clients. Because the practice of law involves any and all subject matters, any trade that you have learned, or skill that you have acquired can probably be used to enhance your marketability in the legal profession so that you will be a more desirable candidate than those with no experience, depending upon an employer's particular needs and preferences.

GETTING IN AND MOVING UP

If you want to help people and promote justice, a professional legal career may be for you. Characteristics of a successful legal professional include

1. a penchant for working pursuant to rules.
2. a desire to bring honor to the profession.
3. a love of reading, writing, and analyzing.
4. superb attention to detail.
5. nerves of steel with perseverance to match.
6. the ability to multitask.
7. amazing communication skills.

Legal professionals should constantly strive to increase their credentials, even if unemployed. The higher the salary you seek, the longer it usually takes to find employment. The most important activities you should participate in are those that will increase your marketability. Activities to consider participating in while looking for employment, include

- contract work.

- political work.

- law-related volunteer work.

- writing articles and other publication efforts.

- temporary work.

- classes on law-related software.

- networking.

- attendance at political, alumni, and charity galas.

- involvement in professional association activities.

- continuing education classes.

- investigating whether alternative education may be of use.

As a legal professional you should utilize your free time so that you are able to foster your professional development. You should have the goals and objectives during your first four years in the profession that may include the following, which should be tailored to your particular profession:

YEAR ONE

- Learn about your legal community, key players, applicable state laws, and licensure requirements.

- Take courses part time to hone up on the skills you will need to be a success in your profession.

- Increase your computer proficiency.

- Learn all you can about your employer and its employees. Review all manuals and policy memos.

- Invest in literature and courses regarding time management. If you must generate billable hours, then budget them and monitor your progress over the year.

- Organize your calendar and telephone directory.

- Decorate your office and acquire an appropriate wardrobe.

- Read any literature or periodicals or newspapers related to your employment. *This should include a subscription to the state bar journal* and any other trade journals or journals that relate to the areas of law with which you must deal.

- Read and subscribe to one or two publications covering news of your profession.

- Investigate certification opportunities for your profession and strive toward attaining certifications.

- Volunteer to assist at firm functions, bar functions, and with other legal organizations in your community.

- Join any local and national professional organizations applicable to your job.

- Volunteer to do research, design, or drafting for the firm newsletter.

YEAR TWO

- Acquire at least one certification and take more courses applicable to the specifics of your profession.

- Learn client operations and procedures and read about industry developments to keep current.

- Enhance or continue the prior year's activities.

YEAR THREE

- Add to your volunteer activities and seek board memberships.

- Join another organization in the area of your specialization.

- Acquire an additional certification.

- Complete a two-year associate program this year related to your profession.

- Enhance or continue prior years' activities.

YEAR FOUR

- Serve on a committee of a professional organization.

- Write an article in your specialty.

- Plan to add another professional committee or take more responsibility for your current one in the next year.

- Write for the firm newsletter.

- Volunteer to be a mentor for a new staff member.

- Reevaluate your career options and where you are headed.

- Evaluate the status of your educational endeavors and finish the acquisition of a degree.

- Enhance or continue prior years' activities.

A FEW KEY POINTS TO REMEMBER

• Before committing to a legal education or career, get some experience and training through curriculum courses and extracurricular activities, internships, temporary work, and volunteer activities.

• Use your past employment history or training to your benefit.

• While employed and unemployed, use your free time to gain more experience and familiarity with your legal community and increase your marketability.

CHAPTER THREE

Legal Secretary

L egal secretaries manage most of the communications their attorneys have. They are somewhat like minimanagers of the attorneys they work for, yet they are also subject to their control, supervision, and direction. On one hand, legal secretaries are eventually given broad responsibilities and control to handle all administrative aspects of their attorney's practice and expected to anticipate their needs; on the other hand, legal secretaries must perform the tasks delegated to them by their attorneys and possibly others. For this reason, in addition to the legal expertise required, legal secretaries earn more on the average than any other type of secretary. The faster legal secretaries can type, the greater their proficiency with word processing, and the better their ability to anticipate attorney needs, the greater the likelihood of advancement and promotional opportunities or landing the secretarial dream job.

THE RIGHT STUFF

Legal secretaries' work is highly specialized and tailored to the legal profession compared to other nonlaw-related secretarial jobs. Legal secretaries should be especially tactful in their dealings with people, who are often frantic and emotional. Interpersonal skills, discretion, good judgment, organizational ability, and initiative are especially important hiring and promotional considerations for law firms. In order to achieve proficiency in a career as a legal secretary, you should acquire competency in

- grammar

- spelling

- punctuation

- keyboarding

- word processing

- database and file management

- e-mail.

If you cannot efficiently organize and prioritize your own assignments, you will not be able to achieve the larger objective—the efficient administrative operation of your firm or organization. You must be sure that your attorneys are free to be able to spend a full day on legal work and generating new clients, and you should strive to ensure that attorneys spend as little time as possible on administrative matters. Supervising attorneys usually depend upon their legal secretaries so they can address their clients' needs in a timely and organized fashion. With keen insight and judgment, legal secretaries can anticipate the needs of attorneys.

WHAT LEGAL SECRETARIES DO

Legal secretaries are responsible for a variety of administrative and clerical duties necessary to maintain a law office.

- They must make sure the work product is completed.

- They provide information when they answer and screen telephone calls and answer or direct other internal inquiries.

- They review all incoming mail, faxes, and docket appearances.

- They make travel and meeting arrangements, and disseminate this information.

- They ensure that the attorneys know where they are supposed to be and when.

- They have all documents prepared that the attorneys need to take with them to meetings or court.

- They type information provided by attorneys or clients from handwritten or electronic drafts or dictation.

- Commonly, legal secretaries complete skeleton blank documents or instruments or forms. As legal secretaries gain experience, attorneys will give them more latitude to deviate from these forms, thereby drafting more original documents, under attorney supervision.

- Every day, legal secretaries ensure that correspondence and other legal documents are finalized, signed, and mailed. Correspondence commonly prepared autonomously by legal secretaries includes transmission letters of documents to clients, opposing counsel, and the court. Often, they transmit questionnaires, interrogatories, and deposition instructions as standard form letters.

- They may assemble records and organize charts, tables of contents, and indexes. Legal secretaries draft correspondences, indices, charts, and tables of contents more often than any other type of document.

- Legal secretaries prepare certificates of mailing for process serving and packages for mailing via the U.S. Post Office or Federal Express. They make sure that all necessary enclosures to correspondence are included, such as copies of certain documents or payments.

- While managing electronic and hard copy files, legal secretaries may also be required to manage projects such as copying and labeling of exhibits for trial or to attach to pleadings.

- Legal secretaries order office supplies, and make sure office equipment is maintained and operational. They may also enter detailed time descriptions and expenses into computer billing systems, and ensure invoices for accounts payable are correct.

Legal secretaries may even perform a multitude of functions outside of those typically associated with their employment, including those of a legal assistant, legal administrator, and legal marketer. Attorneys rely on their legal secretaries to assist with any projects that need to be done, even if the projects involve those outside of normal responsibilities. Because of this, many legal secretaries gain experience in other legal careers and are given an opportunity to move up, if they like. Many times the scope of legal secretarial responsibilities depends upon the size of the office. Generally, the smaller the office, the wider range of job responsibilities they will likely have. Higher-level secretaries tend to perform fewer clerical tasks than lower-level secretaries. Additional responsibilities they may have include conducting research, preparing statistical reports, training employees, and supervising other clerical staff.

WHAT THE JOB IS *REALLY* LIKE

Legal secretaries often sit for long periods of time and usually work 40-hour workweeks. Entry-level secretaries will likely have to work much more. Some legal secretaries have flexible working arrangements that may involve part-time or temporary positions or sharing a position with another secretary. One out of five secretaries works part time but the majority of legal secretaries are full-time employees who work in excess of 40 hours.

Jean Benzel, a legal secretary, says a typical day for her is as follows: "I have a $37\frac{1}{2}$-hour workweek, and rarely work more than 40 hours a week unless I am helping attorneys prepare for trial. I arrive at 8:00 or 8:15 A.M. in order to prepare for my shift that begins at 8:30 A.M. I work $7\frac{1}{2}$-hour days.

"Every night, late-working attorneys prepare assignments for me that wait on my desk. I review e-mail correspondence, voice mails, and my new assignments, then, I begin to complete my assignments. Generally, my assignments involve heavy typing and word processing. I prepare correspondence, pleadings, memorandums, discoveries, and subpoenas. I maintain files, take care of time and billing entries, and proofread all of it.

"I answer the telephone and facilitate communications between attorneys and clients or other persons. Because the attorneys for whom I work specialize in employment and labor law, I may also type grievances and Equal Employment Opportunity Commission complaints. My job is to ensure that the day goes smoothly for the two attorneys who supervise me.

"Overall, a legal secretary's work is never done."

A Person Who's Done It

MEET JEAN BENZEL

VITAL STATISTICS

Jean Benzel changed her career midlife due to a foot operation that required her to sit while working. She is 51 years old and has worked for the past 6 years as a legal secretary with the same attorneys. Her prior work history consists of one year employment as a legal secretary 30 years ago, with 2 years subsequent experience as a corporate secretary, customer service representative, and credit department clerk. After these occupations she became a full-time mom and had a home-based business for ten years.

She worked at a grocery store as a cashier and department supervisor for 10 years until she had a foot operation. Her operation prevented her from being able to continue in her job since she could no longer work standing on her feet for long periods of time. She knew her office skills were not up to par due to increased computer technology, so she enrolled in courses designed to improve her office skills. Then she enrolled in and completed a two-year legal secretarial program at a local junior college. Her first semester in school, she successfully completed an eight-hour exam for her certification as a legal secretary.

She is a member of NALS® . . . the association for legal professionals, a national association for legal professionals that provides her with educational resources and networking opportunities, and has an Accredited Legal Secretary (ALS) and a Certified Professional Legal Secretary (PLS). She also belongs to a local organization that provides resources and networking attorneys for legal secretaries. Here is her story.

I believe that legal secretaries are the top of the line of all secretaries because of the professionalism and work ethic required. My career is a respected one, regardless of whether I call myself an administrative assistant or secretary. The legal secretarial field is not for those who simply want to serve their time and receive a paycheck. It is one that demands hard work and professionalism. If you have these qualities, you will help make up for a shortage of qualified legal secretaries, and if you have a strong work ethic, you will soon make as much money as any college graduate.

In addition to having a strong work ethic, legal secretaries should have a great sense of responsibility and confidentiality. They should plan on at least a full workday and be able to organize, prioritize, and delegate. Legal secretaries should be able to learn something new every day and adapt their skills and proficiencies with changes in technology and job responsibilities.

Legal secretaries should be able to do some legal assistant-type work from time to time, if required. My duties sometimes overlap with those of a paralegal and I am continuing in my educational pursuits to help assist me with these duties. Because I prepare so many pleadings and legal documents, I already have an acquired skill required for the work of a paralegal. By having the ability to perform the duties of a legal secretary and paralegal, I can increase my value to my firm, even though I prefer to remain primarily a secretary. However, with paralegal training, I can be billed out as a paralegal from time to time, as necessity dictates.

I recommend that all aspiring and current legal secretaries pursue education to increase their legal knowledge and skills. Legal secretaries should have excellent grammar, punctuation, and spelling, along with computer proficiency; they should take classes to develop these abilities, if needed. Most attorneys are happy to help you learn what you need to know about the law, but you should have basic skills before embarking on such a career.

Job satisfaction in your employment is most important. Working as a legal secretary is not always a picnic, but your rewards are seeing the end result of your product and contribution to the team effort. Many people think they can't advance and earn a living without a college degree—this is simply not true.

GETTING IN AND MOVING UP

People gain their first job as a legal secretary after
1. working a lower-level job as a receptionist, runner, or file clerk.
2. acquiring an education that prepares them for legal secretarial services.
3. having nonlaw-related secretarial experience.
4. gaining entry into the profession with no experience whatsoever.

Most legal secretaries gain experience on the job and through employer-funded education. The acquisition of a degree or secretarial accreditation while engaged in full-time service is usually the quickest way to increase salary or receive a promotion.

High school graduates who have basic office skills may qualify for entry-level secretarial positions. Employers require knowledge of software applications that most high schools offer. Many legal employers will find knowledge of basic computer operations a great relief and incentive to hire you, as it will decrease the time required to train you.

If you have no computer skills, you should acquire them first to increase your proficiency in keyboarding, spelling, punctuation, grammar, and oral communication. Training may also be obtained from the courses offered at a vocational education program that teaches office skills and keyboarding. Many temporary agencies provide training in computer and office skills. Other specialized training programs exist for legal secretaries, as well; however, legal secretarial skills are most often acquired, through on-the-job instruction. Many secretarial programs may be completed while working as a secretary, or partially completed while still in high school.

Entry-level legal secretarial certifications are available through the International Association of Administrative Professionals and NALS® . . . the association for legal professionals. The International Association of Administrative Professionals offers testing and certification for entry-level office skills and is available through their Office Proficiency Assessment and Certification program. Similarly, those without experience who want to be certified as a legal support professional may be certified as an Accredited Legal Secretary (ALS) by the Certifying Board of NALS® . . . the association for legal professionals. For further information on these organizations, see pages 33–34.

As you gain experience as a secretary, you can earn the Certified Professional Secretary (CPS) designation by meeting certain experience requirements and passing an examination with the International Association of Administrative Professionals. NALS® . . . the association for legal professionals administers an examination to certify a legal secretary with three years of experience as a Professional Legal Secretary (PLS). Further, Legal Secretaries International confers the designation Board Certified Civil Trial Legal Secretary in such specialized areas of law as litigation, real estate, probate, and corporate law. This designation is conferred upon legal secretaries who pass an examination and have at least five years of law-related experience.

Secretaries generally advance by being promoted to other secretarial positions with more responsibilities. Qualified legal secretaries who broaden their knowledge of a firm's operations and enhance their skills may be promoted to other positions such as senior or executive secretary, clerical supervisor, or office manager. With additional training, many legal secretaries become paralegals or enter into other legal professions.

As a legal secretary you must have positive performance reviews and interact well with other staff members and attorneys in order to move ahead in your career within a particular firm or organization. Your performance is judged, in part, by the ability to move work product and handle administrative matters with little or no attorney involvement.

EMPLOYMENT FORECAST

Job openings should be plentiful for legal secretaries. In 1998, 9 percent of all secretaries worked as legal secretaries. Rapid growth in the legal field should lead to average growth for legal secretaries; however, employment of secretaries who do not specialize in legal or medical work is expected to remain flat. From 1998 to 2000 the average annual job openings for legal secretaries was approximately 44,000 jobs a year. From 1998 to 2008 the number of legal secretarial positions is expected to grow from 285,000 jobs to 322,000 jobs. The unemployment rate for legal secretaries will be low.

Growing levels of office automation and organizational restructuring will impact legal secretaries' scope of responsibilities. Increased office automation will make legal secretaries and attorneys more productive. Attorneys continue to develop the ability to complete their own word processing, and legal secretaries are continuing to play an ever-increasing role in editing as their typing and processing duties decline. As office automation increases, organizational restructuring is likely to occur; other workers will assume more secretarial duties due to increased proficiency in office automation so attorneys will more often share secretaries. The traditional arrangement of one secretary per attorney is becoming less prevalent. Instead, legal secretaries increasingly support practice groups, which increases their value as team players.

However, many secretarial duties cannot be automated because they are of a personal, interactive nature. Responsibilities such as planning conferences, working with clients, and transmitting staff instructions require tact and communication skills. Because technology cannot substitute for these personal skills, secretaries will continue to play a key role in most organizations and firms.

EARNINGS

The median base salary for legal secretaries is $15.88 to $21.62 an hour, depending on geographic location. In 1998 median annual earnings of legal secretaries were $30,050. Salaries for legal secretaries generally tend to be higher than other secretarial fields. Earnings vary depending upon skill and responsibility. Entry-level legal secretarial positions tend to average $20,000 to $25,000 a year in most areas of the country. In major metropolitan areas such as the East and West Coasts, average earnings exceed $30,000 per year.

According to Jean Benzel, legal secretaries in the Midwest with no experience generally start out earning $18,000 a year. They earn as much as new attorneys, after five years of experience. For top experience, legal secretaries are paid approximately $35,000 a year in the Midwest. Obviously, one's geographic region in the United States may cause this figure to *drastically* increase or decrease. Small firms tend to pay less without benefits, but a small-firm environment could better suit one's preferences.

PROFESSIONAL CONNECTIONS

International Association of Administrative Professionals (IAAP)
10502 NW Ambassador Drive
P.O. Box 20404
Kansas City, MO 64195-0404
Tel: (816) 891-6600
Fax: (816) 891-9118
E-mail: *exec.director@iaap-hq.org*
Web Site: *http://www.iaap-hq.org*

Legal Secretaries International
8902 Sunnywood Drive
Houston, TX 77088-3729
Tel: (281) 847-9754
Fax: (281) 847-2121
E-mail: *cawilson@compuserve.com*
Web: *http://www.compassnet/legalsec*

NALS® . . . the association for legal professionals
314 East 3rd Street, Suite 210
Tulsa, OK 74120
Tel: (918) 582-5188
Fax: (918) 582-5907
E-mail: *info@nals.org*
Web Site: *http://www.nals.org*

A FEW KEY POINTS TO REMEMBER

- You should have excellent communication and interpersonal skills in order to deal with high-maintenance attorneys, clients, and fellow staff members. Legal secretaries should be "people persons."

- You should generally have a more proficient knowledge of computers and word processing than any other employee of a legal organization.

- You should have a strong work ethic and commitment to your profession.

- You should remain true to your profession and yourself, instead of excessive doting on bosses. By remaining true to your profession and self, you will be a professional asset to your firm.

- You should be loyal to your attorneys, which means not trying to "outshine" them and maintaining confidentiality.

- You should be prepared for a future redistribution of responsibilities assigned to you, and be able to adapt your skills and proficiencies as needed.

CHAPTER FOUR

Legal Assistant

If you would like to be an attorney, but do not want approximately $100,000 to $250,000 of educational debt, seven years of the post-high school education required to obtain a law license, or to litigate in front of jurors and the court, then you should seriously consider a career as a legal assistant. Legal assistants usually work long hours as do attorneys, meticulously research and draft pleadings and other documents, handle client inquiries, and are intimately familiar with all aspects of an attorney's caseload. Legal assistants may be referred to as paralegals or legal assistants, depending on their geographical location or employer's preference. Legal assistants differ from legal secretaries in their substantive knowledge of the law. After acquiring the requisite training on the job or education at a junior college or vocational school, you can become a paralegal or legal assistant. With five years experience, a legal assistant can make more money than many new attorneys and draft all the same documents that attorneys do.

Of all the careers in law that do not require a college degree, the job description of a legal assistant is closest to that of an attorney. Here is a test to see if you are cut out for this profession. The National Federation of Paralegal Associations (NFPA) defines a paralegal as follows:

> [A] person qualified through education, training or work experience, to perform substantive legal work that requires knowledge of legal concepts and is customarily, but not exclusively, performed by a lawyer. This person may be retained or employed by a lawyer, law office, governmental agency, or other entity or may be authorized by administrative, statutory or court authority to perform this work.

Did you take the time to review each word in that definition and its meaning to gain a true insight into what a legal assistant does? If you want to be a legal assistant, you must be able to exercise the time and patience required to understand definitions, legal statutes, and case law. This understanding can be acquired only through training, patience, and careful attention to detail.

THE RIGHT STUFF

Legal assistants are empowered with great responsibility to help the attorneys for whom they work complete paper-intensive legal tasks. They should have a keen eye for detail when reviewing stacks of documents and should be able to organize voluminous records and summarize critical issues and facts by referring to those documents. If you have substantive legal knowledge and the ability to perform competent, thorough, and efficient legal research, you will perform well as a legal assistant. Through the continuous review of case law and statutes, you should remain knowledgeable about the ever-changing nature of the law. Legal analysis requires application of facts to the law in each client's case or a discussion of what facts make the case an exception to a law's application.

Careful attention to policies, rules, and regulations, and the exact wording contained therein, is a must in the legal profession. You should be able to rebut in writing the arguments made by opposing counsel, and support their arguments. Your written communication skills should be excellent. If you like to read and write and are good at research and writing, you are likely to do well. Practical experience, familiarity with legal terminology, and good investigative skills are all advantages.

You should be able to act as a legal liaison between clients and attorneys. If a client is unable to reach the attorney, he or she will try to contact you first for answers to law-related questions. You should be familiar with the attorney's caseload in order to effectively address client concerns and have the judgment and insight to know when you should not, in order to avoid the unauthorized practice of law. Good legal assistants will not try to outshine the attorneys for whom they work and will try to complement the services the attorney provides. Legal assistants should have excellent interpersonal skills and oral communication skills. Productivity is critical. They should exceed billing requirements even if they have had a leave of absence. They should be well-liked, positive people, satisfied with their positions, and confident in their abilities.

Successful legal assistants pay close attention to the quality of their work product, even if they are under a deadline. Your work as a legal assistant should be the best it can be with no grammar, punctuation, or spelling errors, and you should be consistently on time.

Annetta Smith, legal assistant, notes that attorneys currently bear the brunt of discipline and responsibility for a legal assistant's work. Attorneys should advise legal assistants of the attorney's ethical obligations to which their employees are bound. A successful legal assistant will know what the attorney's code of professional responsibility requires and abide by it.

WHAT LEGAL ASSISTANTS DO

Before you learn what people in your prospective profession actually do, you should know the many laws regarding what legal assistants *cannot* do. Because legal assistants perform so many of the same tasks as attorneys, strict regulations and laws govern their actions. These are increasing. State law and bar associations are committed to preventing the unauthorized practice of law, and many cases and statutes interpret exactly what the unauthorized practice of law is. Generally, laws preclude legal assistants from giving legal advice, having personal conferences with clients, advertising professional guidance, or advising clients about proper testimony. In addition, legal assistants may not, generally, do the following:

1. define concepts and legal terms of art to clients
2. render advice peculiar to a client's situation
3. use their judgment to determine which client questions to answer themselves and which to refer to the attorney
4. sign retention letters
5. add language not dictated by a client or attorney
6. provide others with documents prepared by an attorney or otherwise published to assist the person in representing himself or herself in a contested matter

Legal assistants are confronted daily with requests to commit the unauthorized practice of law from clients, telephone inquiries, and sometimes even unknowing attorneys. It is the attorney's responsibility to supervise all the legal assistant's work to prevent the unauthorized practice of law. An attorney may delegate tasks to legal assistants, as long as they maintain direct relationships with their clients and remain responsible for the work product. Legal assistants should be familiar with their local and state laws regarding what they can and cannot do in order to avoid the unauthorized practice of law.

Legal assistants perform a multitude of functions depending on their employer's preference. These functions may encompass exclusively attorney-related tasks such as drafting pleadings, or they may include other tasks commonly handled by secretarial or other personnel. Docketing and scheduling are very important tasks for legal assistants that require careful attention to detail and knowledge of the legal rules regarding response times. After all, failure to correctly docket deadlines and schedule meetings could result in a legal malpractice suit.

DOCUMENTS

Generally, legal assistants exclusively help attorneys complete all document-related legal tasks. They perform preparatory work to uncover all facts of a case, and they research relevant law. A significant portion of most legal assistants' work involves drafting documents for litigation and memorandum opinions. When they prepare legal memorandum opinions they are assisting attorneys with strategy decisions. The opinion they draft could have to do with any area of the law and may be utilized in future pleadings or client correspondence. Legal assistants who do not work in a litigation department, may draft other types of legal documents depending on their firm's practice. Other types of documents may include contracts, mortgages, trusts, wills, abstracts, separation agreements, corporate minutes, and articles of incorporation.

PETITIONS

The most commonly prepared documents are pleadings for filing with a court clerk. What legal assistants draft will largely depend upon whether the firm or organization represents the plaintiff or defendant in a case or must file a motion or oppose one. Documents for litigation may be based on a firm's standard forms or created from scratch. Usually, the first pleading drafted for a plaintiff is the petition or complaint. In order to draft an effective petition, legal assistants should determine with the help of their supervising attorney whether the pleading is one that is likely to be subject to a motion to dismiss or is particularly complicated in any regard. If it is, then great detail and time should be invested in the drafting of the petition to avoid the unnecessary expenditure of time required to respond to a motion to dismiss. Legal assistants will need to use all preliminary fact gathering and research to draft such a petition. Other petitions may simply involve the completion of a standardized or sample petition with a new case style and other facts inserted where appropriate.

Defense legal assistants will have to determine whether or not to file a motion to dismiss based upon a petition, or simply file an answer. Motions to dismiss are critical considerations since, if granted, some or all of a plaintiff's claims will be dismissed.

DISCOVERY

Once this stage is complete, discovery commences. Written discovery entails the formulation and answering of interrogatories, which are a series of questions that a legal assistant may answer with an attorney and client's assistance. Written discovery also involves the preparation and responses to requests for production that simply require that all evidence or other documents regarding the claims or defenses in litigation be produced. Legal assistants may also need to formulate or answer requests for admission that require a party to admit or deny that certain facts are true. If any interrogatories, requests for production, or requests for admission are not answered, then the litigants must generally prepare correspondence to resolve the issues in good faith. If the parties cannot resolve any written discovery disputes, then motions to compel or subpoenas must be issued.

EXHIBITS AND WITNESSES FOR DEPOSITION AND TRIAL

A legal assistant must identify likely exhibits and witnesses for deposition and trial. The supervising attorney will choose who he or she wants to depose on the opposing party's side. Once depositions are complete, the legal assistant will prepare deposition summaries and perform any follow-up written discovery requests needed.

MOTIONS FOR SUMMARY JUDGMENT

Any party to litigation may file a motion for summary judgment based on the evidence. Such a motion simply requests that the court rule in a party's favor without trial because under no set of facts could a party's claims or defenses be proven to be true and entitle them to judgment. A motion for summary judgment is generally the most comprehensive brief that addresses the law and all facts of a case. Discovery efforts are often directed at overcoming the summary judgment obstacle before trial.

PRETRIAL CONFERENCE ORDERS, MOTIONS IN LIMINE, AND SUBPOENAS

Before trial, legal assistants prepare pretrial conference orders that list all witnesses and exhibits, and address other trial matters in coordination with opposing counsel. They must also prepare and respond to motions in limine that state objections to evidence and deposition testimony being admitted at trial. Finally, legal assistants may prepare proposed jury instructions, if needed, and issue subpoenas for witness testimony. Other motions and pleadings are also generally required, but these are the basic tasks legal assistants must learn to perform. Most firms have comprehensive samples that legal assistants can use as a guideline and attorneys are available to help legal assistants draft these pleadings.

Every jurisdiction has different requirements for the filing and timing of legal documents. This is meant to be only a general guideline and is not indicative of the law in a particular area.

WHAT THE JOB IS *REALLY* LIKE

A typical day for a legal assistant begins with a review of the docket. The docket is usually a bound calendar in which legal assistants, secretaries, and attorneys enter deadlines for the completion of projects, court appearances, and meetings. As a legal assistant you should ensure that your projects are completed on time and that docket entries are correct. It is of particular importance that you double-check any docket entries of secretaries or other support staff. When you review the docket, you should search several months in advance to make sure documents are completed on time. Research regarding filing deadlines is a common necessity to avoid the negative consequences of failing to file timely court documents. You should then organize your personal calendar to reflect a personal deadline for completing all assigned tasks, and to serve as reminders to attorneys of any impending deadlines.

According to Annetta Smith, "A typical day for me begins at 7:45 A.M. and ends at 7:00 P.M. I perform support services for three attorneys at my firm and docket, organize, and prioritize my assignments and the schedules of the attorneys. My assignments include: handling all aspects of discovery, including document production, interrogatories, and requests for production; review of factual documents pertaining to cases; locating witnesses for interview; drafting pleadings and motions; review of depositions; and preparation of direct and cross-examination questions. I handle all aspects of cases from initial client contact to trial preparation and participation."

A Person
Who's Done It

MEET ANNETTA SMITH, CDT/ALS/CPLS

VITAL STATISTICS

Annetta Smith is a 36-year-old legal assistant with McKinney & Stringer, P.C., where she specializes in employment law, business litigation, product liability, and general insurance defense. She has been in law-related careers for the past 15 years.

Annetta has a variety of skills that have helped her in her successful legal career. She is proficient in Microsoft Windows 97, Outlook, Schedule Plus, Power Point, Word, and Works. She knows billing applications such as Juris and Timeslips and is also proficient in Microsoft database management in Imanage, Soft Solutions, Excel, and Access. She is competent in Internet Explorer and electronic mail.

Annetta has had 14 articles published regarding the paralegal profession, professionalism, and leadership, and has received numerous awards for her professional contributions. She received her associate degree with a certificate in legal secretary studies and holds professional certifications as a Certified Diversity Trainer (CDT), Accredited Legal Secretary (ALS), and Certified

Professional Legal Secretary (CPLS). She has authored and presented legal training courses and professional development seminars for various legal professional associations in eight states and is a member of the National Federation of Paralegal Associations (NFPA), National Notary Association (NNA), The Professional Woman Network (PWN), and NALS® . . . the association for legal professionals. She is currently serving as a member of the advisory boards for two vocational schools. Here is her story.

I graduated from high school in 1982 with honors and dreams of becoming a Certified Public Accountant. I went to college on an accounting scholarship. In the spring of 1983 I became pregnant and was unsure about my future. I spoke to a guidance counselor about my need to earn a living to take care of my child as a single parent. My guidance counselor suggested I change my career goals from accounting to legal secretarial studies. I was told that the legal secretarial profession is a respected one and that with a two-year degree I could earn a living to take care of my child. In the summer of 1985 I graduated with a certificate in legal secretarial studies.

Immediately following graduation, I relocated to California where I was hired by a respected firm for my first job as a legal secretary. This was a very proud moment for me and my boss taught me everything about being a legal secretary that I was not taught in school. I learned how important professionalism, work ethic, integrity, and respect for my chosen profession is. Fifteen years later, this boss is still my mentor and friend.

In 1999 I became a nationally accredited legal secretary through NALS® . . . the association for legal professionals. This increased my knowledge and experience in law office management, legal principles, written communications, ethics and judgment, and legal research and writing. I am currently enrolled in Kaplan College in correspondence courses to acquire my degree in paralegal studies. My anticipated graduation date is in 2001 and the courses will take me three years to complete. I have taken a variety of other courses through NALS® . . . the association for legal professionals to increase my expertise and knowledge in all areas of the law. Continuing legal education is just as important as typing speed.

As a legal secretary I was delegated the responsibilities of a legal assistant, such as legal research, drafting of state and federal lawsuits, drafting discovery pleadings, and assisting in document productions. Then, from January 1990 through December 1994, I worked in California as an executive director/legal assistant for an educational resource firm that presented continuing legal education seminars to legal professionals.

As an executive director, my job responsibilities were most similar to that of a legal marketing professional, but also included responsibilities of a legal administrator and legal assistant. I planned and implemented marketing campaigns, acted as chief company spokesperson, supervised events and publications, and prepared press releases and public relations materials. I also developed, planned, coordinated, organized, and presented CLE seminars and workshops. I assisted with fiscal planning and budgeting, the supervision of personnel, prepared reports and policy statements, and developed training manuals.

From 1995 through 1997 I worked exclusively as a paralegal/legal secretary for a well-respected law firm. Then, in 1997 I accepted my current position with McKinney & Stringer, P.C. as a legal assistant.

GETTING IN AND MOVING UP

Computer technology has decreased the time required for legal research. Instead of poring over volumes of research material in law libraries, you can access the same information more and more efficiently as technology advances. You should be able to increase your computer and research proficiency along with technological advances in order to advance in your profession as a legal assistant.

Many legal assistants enter the profession after completing American Bar Association-approved college or training programs, or are trained on the job by legal employers. Although most legal assistant programs are completed in two years with the acquisition of an associate degree in Arts or Science

(A.A. or A.S.), a growing number of colleges and universities offer four-year bachelor's degree programs with a bachelors degree in Arts or Science (B.A. or B.S.) in paralegal studies. The Certified Legal Assistant (CLA) designation conferred by the National Association of Legal Assistants will greatly enhance employment opportunities. In order to move up in your career, you should continue to acquire education, if you have not already done so.

Certain practical skills courses should be taken by legal assistants. These include Pretrial Practice and Procedure, Trial Practice and Procedure, Appellate Practice and Procedure, and Research and Writing. Other substantive legal courses in your firm's area of specialization will also increase a legal assistant's value to a firm and help a legal assistant to get ahead.

BRIEF WRITING

If you are detail-oriented with a creative flair at just the right moment, you may be well suited for a legal assistant career. A legal assistant must exercise sound discretion and judgment when exercising creativity in brief writing. Creative flair is not always appreciated but judges who are bored reading the same old briefs, appellate courts that want to know why they should change precedent, or clients with great convictions about their cases, may appreciate it. Your ability to creatively address issues will also be directed by your employer's preferences. You should not get too creative at first until you learn the ropes and your employer's preference.

If the position is one that may require the submission of a writing sample, you should review and revise your collection of samples, paying particular attention to logic flow, citations, and sentence structure. Do not hesitate to use boldface, italics, and underlining in legal briefs and other writing samples. You should have several writing samples that will appeal to a variety of different employers.

INTERNSHIPS

In order to gain experience in this field, you may want to consider an internship. Fifty percent of paralegal internships are offered by private firms; banks, insurance companies, corporations, government, and others offer internships as well. If you decide to look for an internship, particularly if it is with employers that may not already have an established internship program, you must not only sell your personality and skills, but you must also sell the idea of an internship itself to a potential internship sponsor.

TIME

Time and expenses should be recorded on a pad at least once an hour or directly into a program such as Timeslips. No one who records eight billable hours in an eight and one-half-hour workday is being honest; six or seven billable hours is more likely. A list of deadlines should be carefully maintained, and referred to daily in order to prioritize assignments. Legal professionals should create memorandums of discussion points with others and clients should be advised in a timely way of all developments in a case.

In assigning work, a partner may seem indifferent to the time needed for its completion and may fail to specify a deadline. It should be assumed that every assignment of work requires immediate or almost immediate performance. Local court rules should be consulted to ensure timely filing of pleadings.

The first two years after entry into the legal assistant profession are most critical. In order to get into this profession you should be willing to work up to 90 hours a week, if necessary, for at least two years. After five years' experience, a legal assistant should have significantly more responsibility and less supervision, possibly even supervisory responsibilities, with fewer work hours. If a legal assistant is confined in career opportunities with the employer, he or she may find better advancement opportunities by changing employers.

EMPLOYMENT FORECAST

Much of the groundwork now covered by the legal assistant was once within the attorney's domain. The work of the legal assistant allows attorneys to focus more on case strategy and the resolution of legal problems. Traditional legal assistants usually work for law offices, corporations, government agencies, or other legal entities. Contract legal assistants perform paralegal work on a case-by-case basis and usually possess many years of paralegal experience or specialized expertise. Independent legal assistants generally perform work directly to consumers in such matters as uncontested divorces.

Between 1998 and 2008 the number of legal assistant positions is expected to grow 62 percent from 136,000 to 220,000. With the increased demand for legal services and the emergence of prepaid legal insurance plans that allow more of the public access to attorneys, it can be expected that the demand for legal assistants will increase. A large number of men comprise the 129,630 legal assistants reported in the United States; some statistics show that 70 percent of this number is male.

EARNINGS

On the average, legal assistants work 40 hours a week, but entry-level legal assistants tend to work twice as much. The average starting salary is $21,000, but after five years' experience, the average salary increases to $31,700. With 10 to 15 years of experience you can expect to earn in excess of $40,000. A 1995 Findings of Paralegal Compensation and Benefits Survey revealed the average legal assistant salary to be $32,875. Further, according to the Association of Legal Administrators, the hourly rate for legal assistants is between $18.17 and $23.73 an hour. In order to anticipate what your earnings are likely to be, you should consider your geographic location and the size of the firm for which you work.

Many states consider legislation that would allow legal assistants to share in attorney fees and contingency fee compensation. Currently, legal assistants cannot receive compensation as attorneys. This means that even if you bill your time at $75 an hour with 160 hours a month, you cannot share in a percentage of the $12,000 charge to the client, nor can you share in a percentage of a contingency fee case. Contingency fee cases generally require that the client agree that 25 to 50 percent of any monies received from their case be paid directly to the attorney as compensation. In exchange, an attorney will usually advance all costs for a client and not charge attorney fees. In this scenario, if the client's case is lost, no attorney fees or costs will be owed by the client. The attorney's professional rules of conduct generally prohibit non-attorneys to share in legal fees earned. This means that a salary or hourly rate should be paid to a legal assistant regardless of the income the billable hours generate unless legislation is passed that allows otherwise.

PROFESSIONAL CONNECTIONS

American Association for Paralegal Education (AAFPE)
2965 Flowers Road S, Suite 105
Atlanta, GA 30341-5520
Tel: (770) 452-9877
Fax: (770) 458-3314
E-mail: *sabanske@aol.com*

American Bar Association
Standing Committee on Legal Assistants
750 North Lake Shore Drive
Chicago, IL 60611
E-mail: *legalassts@abanet.org*
Web Site: *http://www.abanet.org/legalassts*

Legal Assistant Management Association (LAMA)
2965 Flowers Road S, Suite 105
Atlanta, GA 30341
Tel: (770) 457-7746
Fax: (770) 458-3314
E-mail: *lamaoffice@aol.com*
Web Site: *http://www.lamanet.org*

National Association of Legal Assistants, Inc.
1516 South Boston Avenue, Suite 200
Tulsa, OK 74119
Tel: (918) 587-6828
Fax: (918) 582-6772
E-mail: *nalanet@nala.org*
Web Site: *http://www.nala.org*

National Federation of Paralegal Associations (NFPA)
$^c/_o$ Lu Hangley
P.O. Box 33108
Kansas City, MO 64114-0108
Tel: (816) 941-4000
Fax: (816) 941-2725
E-mail: *info@paralegals.org.*
Web Site: *http://www.paralegals.org*
Offers the Paralegal Advanced Competency Examination (PACE).

National Paralegal Association
Box 406
Solebury, PA 18963
Tel: (215) 297-8333
Fax: (215) 297-8358
E-mail: admin@nationalparalegal.org
Web Site: *http://www.nationalparalegal.org/*

A FEW KEY POINTS TO REMEMBER

- The work of the legal assistant is the most demanding of careers discussed in this text because their work most closely resembles that of an attorney.
- Be where you want to be in terms of your employment. If you must, change positions to find the right employer for you who will recognize your achievements.
- You should be able to perform despite exposure to high-stress challenges and be precise and on time.
- You should be able to juggle several tasks at once.

CHAPTER FIVE

Legal Administrator

According to Legal Administrator Jeanne Day: "The best part of my job was implementing an employee recognition program. It makes me feel great about my job when I am able to reward and recognize the hard work and contributions of staff members." Legal administrators address the same issues as managers in other industries, but should have training or experience in professional legal careers. As in other legal professions, the scope of responsibilities among legal administrators may differ. In this career, more than in any of the others in this book, you will see that the highest degree of experience is required, but a college degree is not necessary. Most medium- to large-sized firms have at least one legal administrator, if not several, each with different areas of responsibility. Smaller firms tend to have legal administrators that take on many additional responsibilities of other careers in the law profession discussed in this book.

THE RIGHT STUFF

Legal administrators should be able to handle all administrative aspects of a law office, and exhibit professionalism, decorum, and leadership even in the midst of a crisis. They should follow the instructions of the law firm partners, the firm owner, or board of directors, and implement their requests precisely, even if they disagree with the directives given. Legal administrators should be good listeners who enjoy people with a variety of personalities and are able to focus on people's attributes. A legal administrator should be a multitask person with a positive attitude and good interpersonal skills.

A legal administrator must have the insight and wisdom to understand the workings of the firm she or he is in. When establishing internal controls and interacting with staff it is imperative that legal administrators recognize if their firm is one that rewards strong individualist, secretive, or territorial behavior. If the firm is this type, it will not be able to handle strong internal controls and employee evaluation. Understanding the firm's organizational environment is the key to a legal administrator's effectiveness.

Legal administrators should be able to work with attorneys and other senior staff to form alliances and project teams. This requires that a legal administrator compromise, mediate between warring factions, listen, and respond, instead of react, and foster a strong consultative ethos. They should remain empathetic to employee grievances and strictly adhere to office policies and federal and state laws regarding their grievances. They should be peacemakers and people pleasers and treat their organizations as an internal market with the customers being the staff members. They should be talented in the area of interpersonal relations and communications.

WHAT LEGAL ADMINISTRATORS DO

A legal administrator's duties can include everything from managing human resources to finances to space planning, For example:

- Legal administrators may select and implement employee benefits packages, select office furniture and decor or relocation, or hire new staff.

- Legal administrators investigate different options available for the fulfillment of a particular need, analyze the strengths, weaknesses, and cost efficiency of each, and recommend the best choice.

- Legal administrators manage the staff of a firm. They scrutinize preferred work styles, daily routines, habits, and even temperaments of staff members. They should have operational knowledge of all employees' expertise and competencies.

- They draft and revise employee handbooks and must be intimately familiar with all aspects of the guide.

- They identify issues of concern of staff members, train and develop employee skills, and conduct performance evaluations and salary surveys. Legal administrators are responsible for ensuring that the firm or organization has the right staff with the right stuff at the point of hire and development.

- Legal administrators manage the firm's operation. They generally have a background in accounting in order to address accounts payable, accounts receivable, payroll, and benefits.

- They manage safety and security issues, information systems and technologies, purchasing and logistics, mail room operations, and vendor relations. They also prepare cash flow budgets, establish internal controls, and implement client trust accounts. In order to effectively manage a law office, legal administrators should have experience in many of the positions available in a law firm.

WHAT THE JOB IS *REALLY* LIKE

Attorneys do not have to know how to successfully run a business or even handle trust accounts in order to graduate law school. Attorneys rely on their legal administrators to manage their offices. Legal administrators have a high level of responsibility and pressure to make sure they meet the partners' standards. According to Jeanne Day, a legal administrator, one of the biggest differences between working for a corporation and a law firm is that in a corporation you have one boss, but in a law firm your bosses are each of the individual firm partners—you have to answer to each one of these partners for your actions.

On a typical day, Jeanne Day arrives at the office at 7:30 A.M. and prepares to make her office rounds. "I walk throughout the office and speak with staff members and the attorneys regarding any special needs they have. For example, if a secretary is having a bad day, I ask her why. If she has too much work to complete, then I locate a "floater" to help her complete her assignments. If there are not enough floaters available on a given day, I will personally chip in and help. This is part of being a team player, which my firm emphasizes. While making my rounds, I check the office supplies to make sure they are being ordered when needed.

"Weekly, I review staff time sheets to make sure they are approved and ready for submission. I conduct staff meetings and propose and implement a variety of programs designed to foster the effective administration and management of the firm. Also, I am currently assisting the staff in the creation of a secretarial survival manual that will address all issues relative to the proper completion of their responsibilities. I regularly handle any and all human resource issues that arise, hiring new staff members, and reviewing their performance and complaints.

"Currently, we are remodeling our office so I have to make sure I coordinate the painters' activities in such a way as to cause the least amount of discomfort to the staff as possible. For example, I have persuaded the painters to do their prep work in the afternoons and begin painting in the evening, thus minimizing the staff exposure to fumes. Then I have to send out memos to the staff regarding when to expect the painters' arrivals and clear their desks."

A Person Who's Done It

MEET JEANNE DAY

VITAL STATISTICS

Jeanne began her career as a legal assistant in 1983 and now she is a successful legal administrator for a large law firm. She has a multitude of experience in many of the careers discussed in this text. Jeanne acquired her position with an associate degree in business and much experience and perseverance. She also enjoys being a "people pleaser" and helping staff members so that their day runs smoothly. Here is her story.

I knew I wanted to be a legal administrator after working with two large corporations in their human resources departments handling a variety of legal compliance issues. I began my career assisting human resource directors and learning how to implement employee benefit plans and other employment issues.

As a legal assistant in 1983 I prepared legal documents, scheduled meetings and court appearances, and organized lectures for two years. Then I worked for four years as a legal administrator who maintained accounts receivable and payable, and payroll. I also supervised personnel, prepared legal documents, and performed general legal secretarial services. From 1983 through 1996 I worked for various corporations. My responsibilities included preparation of corporate minutes, human resources and legal issues, supervision of clerical assistants, and public relations.

I continued in this capacity for another year with the additional responsibilities of employee preparation of weekly and monthly goals and objectives, conducting staff meetings, coordination of office relocations, recruiting and terminating staff, recommending image enhancement strategies, and implementing technological advancements in the office. In 1998 I began preparing power point presentations and compiling and preparing spreadsheets for a corporate sales office.

Since 1998 I have worked as the legal administrator for a firm with 280 employees. My prior job responsibilities allowed me to acquire the skills necessary for my current position. I am responsible for hiring and terminating staff, conducting performance reviews, providing management support and guidance for staff, managing and implementing human resource issues such as discrimination, medical insurance, and 401(K) Plans, coordinating office remodeling efforts, and setting a positive and professional example for the staff.

My job requires me to exhibit the image and identity of the firm at all times. I have a positive attitude and seek to generate positive attitudes in the people around me. In order to be a success in this field, you should be a real "people pleaser" and want staff members to have a good day. You should look for the good in all people, even difficult ones. You have to give people the benefit of the doubt and take time to listen to their concerns and consider them. If someone irritates you, you should walk away and address the issue with them at a later time. You should also have the judgment and insight to anticipate the needs of others and prevent partners from placing you in the middle of situations that are not part of your job.

GETTING IN AND MOVING UP

Managing the business affairs of a law firm requires special expertise. Among other things, a legal administrator must remain up to date on new technology, management trends, and changes in the way law practices are structured. Additional education and the acquisition of certifications will help legal administrators to get into their positions and move up. Certifications available that may help legal administrator's increase their value to a firm include Certified Legal Manager (CLM), Certified Employee Benefits Specialist (CEBS), and Certified Human Resource Specialist (CHRS). A legal administrator should also consider additional education and the acquisition of other memberships and certifications that his or her staff members may have.

EMPLOYMENT FORECAST

Legal administrators are primarily employed in private law firms, legal service clinics, corporate and university legal departments, government legal agencies, court systems, charitable legal agencies, or other organizations engaged primarily in the practice of law. Because the legal profession is growing, it is expected that the available legal administrator positions will grow as well.

EARNINGS

Legal administrators are known under different titles and have different areas of responsibility that cause pay rates to vary. According to the ALA:

- A principal legal administrator earns between $67,890 and $80,000 on the average, depending on geographic location. The average median salary for a principal legal administrator with no college education is $65,950.

- An administrative office manager earns between $45,750 and $60,090, depending on geographic location. The average median salary for an administrative office manager with no college is $51,000 a year.

- A human resources director or manager earns between $53,250 and $75,000 a year, depending on geographic location. Without any college, the median salary is $59,500.

- An office services or facilities manager earns between $41,048 and $54,534.

- A benefits administrator or coordinator with no college earns a median salary of $44,300.

PROFESSIONAL CONNECTION

Association of Legal Administrators
175 East Hawthorn Parkway, Suite 325
Vernon Hills, IL 60061-1428
Tel: (847) 816-1212
Fax: (847) 816-1213
E-mail: *webmaster@alanet.org*
Web Site: http://www.alanet.org

A FEW KEY POINTS TO REMEMBER

• As a legal administrator you should have knowledge of employment issues, payroll, and benefits at a minimum, unless an employer is willing to train you for further duties.

• You should have some law office experience.

• You should be an expert at interpersonal communications and be a real "people pleaser."

Legal Marketing Professional

L egal marketing professionals coordinate, direct, and implement a law firm's publicity strategies. Prior to 1977 attorneys, unlike most other professionals, had to adhere to strict restrictions regarding their marketing activities. In 1977 the United States Supreme Court eased these restrictions. Each state currently has different statutory and professional rules of conduct regarding advertising restrictions applied to attorneys and firms. Legal marketing professionals should know these restrictions to be sure their firm does not violate any laws or their professional responsibilities when advertising.

THE RIGHT STUFF

The larger the firm, the more likely it is that its primary legal marketing professional will have a college degree. However, a college degree is not required for many available positions in this field, either as an assistant at a larger firm or as a director or manager in a smaller firm. What is important is that legal marketing professionals have general knowledge regarding law firm operation and maintenance and enthusiasm for legal marketing. Legal marketing professionals should have the ability to generate marketing ideas that anticipate and address a law firm's needs in a cost-effective manner.

As a legal marketing professional, you should have confidence and attention to detail. Long-term vision and perseverance are critical to the recommendation and evaluation of marketing efforts. You should be independent, self-motivated, capable of multiple tasks at a time, and a decision maker. Computer skills in a variety of word processing, graphics design, and spreadsheet software are a necessity.

You should possess impeccable written communication skills and the ability to transform complicated legal lingo into layman's terms. Written communications should be clear, precise, and honest. You should have the judgment and intuition to make definitive decisions on the spot when needed. Your verbal communication skills should be excellent in order to deal with clients and the press, especially if confronted. You should be a good listener and able to communicate one on one and in front of large groups. Effective legal marketing professionals inspire trust, confidence, and motivation in attorneys who have a variety of personality types, communication styles, and practice and development goals. They easily manage and face stress.

WHAT LEGAL MARKETING PROFESSIONALS DO

- Legal marketing professionals manage and direct all public relations of a law firm. Public relations includes more than just advertising and promotions. It also includes recommending community involvement and charitable contributions and sponsorships of firm's members and employees, as well as identification of professional development opportunities for attorneys and personnel and ensuring proper client relations and services.

- Legal marketing professionals' public relations endeavors are directed at improving, maintaining, or developing a firm's image. They maintain a firm's image through their conduct with the press, clients, staff, and vendors, and assist other staff members with manifestation of the proper firm image as well.

- Legal marketing professionals manage databases for current, former, and potential clients to receive newsletters, announcements, client surveys, and other promotional activities.

- Legal marketing professionals develop and evaluate client surveys to identify the strengths and weaknesses of their firms, client satisfaction, concerns, and expectations. They also track referral sources of new business and maintain positive relations with these sources.

- Through selection of and contact with graphics designers and desktop publishers, printers, web designers, mail houses, and advertisers, legal marketing professionals coordinate and implement promotional materials. These coordination efforts will require legal marketing professionals to schedule meetings; solicit and evaluate bids for projects; draft, review, and revise ads and tear sheets or other materials; monitor responses and status; report to senior partners; and process invoice payments.

- Legal marketing professionals maintain the firm's biography and investigate and recommend opportunities for employees to improve their credentials. Maintenance of the firm biography will entail arranging for current photographs of firm members, along with each professional's biographical data, including experience, and capabilities; community and professional accomplishments and memberships, and current clients.

- The identification and organization of speaking engagements, seminars, conferences, and continuing legal education classes help attorneys market their services in their areas of specialty. Legal marketing professionals prepare visual and handout materials for these events. They must remain knowledgeable about the activities of attorneys and staff in order to identify and recommend appropriate engagements, as well as publication efforts by attorneys.

- Legal marketing professionals may develop and maintain a firm's Internet presence through web sites or on-line directories. They also compile news reports and prepare press releases on a monthly, annual, or as-needed basis.

WHAT THE JOB IS *REALLY* LIKE

Legal marketing professionals' jobs vary greatly depending on the amount of responsibility they have. The greater the amount of responsibility, the more a legal marketing professional will be able to develop and strategize marketing plans, instead of simply managing and implementing them. Because most employment opportunities available without a college degree will involve reporting to a managing partner, marketing partner, committee, administrator, or executive director, entry-level responsibilities will likely consist of managing and implementing marketing strategies already in place.

According to Mozhgan Mizban, director of client services at Cooley Godward LLP: "In a typical day I start my work in the car on the cell phone. I arrive at work around 9:00 A.M. and work anywhere from an 11- to a 14-hour day. My responsibilities include personnel management, client service, strategic planning, attorney coaching/training, public relations, desktop publishing, identification and promotion of sponsorship opportunities, and much more—variety is the operative word!

"Checking e-mails and voice mails is a regular and constant part of my day. The other constant is meetings. The meetings I attend generally concern marketing strategy and how our firm can implement these strategies. Between meetings, I am consulted on a variety of questions about how to complete pending projects. Also, business and legal reporters call several times a day regarding the best attorney to consult with regarding legal developments and trends.

"I travel regularly; once a year, I travel to London with three partners to participate at a Cooley-sponsored life sciences conference. During this conference we put on a legal workshop for approximately 60 attendees, talk to clients all day, talk to reporters, and host a client dinner for approximately 50 participants. Attorneys, department members, and I travel to a variety of other conferences throughout the year in such places as New York, Washington, D.C., and Santa Barbara, California. Also, I travel approximately twice a year to the Cooley offices outside the Bay Area—we have a total of eight offices— to consult with department members and attorneys on active projects.

"In addition to all this, I conduct client service interviews. This means that I meet with CEOs, General Counsel, and other leading decision makers of corporate clients, and get feedback regarding the quality of service they have received from us. I communicate their feedback—good and bad—to all Cooley client team members and the managing partner of the firm. Department members and I routinely coach attorneys on how to build and maintain professional relationships with clients. Our marketing efforts are not designed to acquire new clients; they are designed to retain and enhance relationships with existing clients."

A Person Who's Done It

MEET MOZHGAN MIZBAN

VITAL STATISTICS

In 1982 Mozhgan Mizban graduated from high school, attended a business college for one year, received a legal diploma, and then accepted her first position as a legal secretary. After three years of experience working as a legal secretary for two partners, she wanted a promotion in her firm as an attorney recruiting manager. She was told that she was too young to assume this position; she was 22. She was not dismayed and persisted for another year and a half in her career until she received a job offer as recruiting director at another firm.

Mozhgan worked at her second law firm as recruiting director and legal secretary for approximately four years before moving on to her third law firm to handle attorney recruiting on a full-time basis. After her first year in this position, Mozhgan's firm created a new position for her in legal marketing where she learned the basics. Subsequently, she received a job offer from a larger firm that already had an established marketing culture. She was very happy with this firm for two years until her current employer made her an offer she couldn't refuse. Now, at the age of 36, Mozhgan is the director of client services *at the law firm of Cooley Godward LLP. Her firm has approximately 700 attorneys with a total of approximately 1,600 employees in 8 different offices across the United States. Mozhgan now manages a department with 20 employees. She and other department members assist the firm's partners in targeting and responding to opportunities for advancement and growth; they are the consultants for the firm's marketing and strategic development efforts. Mozhgan is a critical player and resource for Cooley Godward LLP due to her years of hard work and developed expertise, which cannot be learned in college.*

She is a founding member of the Bay Area Chapter of the Law Firm Marketing Association (LMA/Bay Area) and served as the 1994 president. She has lectured attorneys, in-house counsel, and other marketing professionals on marketing topics such as "How to Build Consensus" and "Client Service Interviews." She has authored articles published in Law Marketing Exchange. *Here is her story.*

In 1982, after I graduated from high school, I attended a business college to learn some basic business skills. I started working full time in 1983. In 1989 I again began working toward a college degree while pursuing my career full time. I received my bachelor's degree in 1998 but by that time, I was so well established in my career that the degree itself did not contribute to my success. The lack of a college degree never held me back. For those with a strong work ethic and supportive mentors, success without a college degree is very achievable.

As a legal secretary in 1983 I produced legal documents, assisted with time entry and billing, and dealt with client concerns. I particularly liked interacting with clients and other people. I wanted a promotion in that firm to attorney recruiting manager, but was turned down due to my young age. I was not deterred and a year and a half later was offered a position with a prior firm partner at his new firm. My employment there began with the joint responsibilities of an assistant and recruiting director. I and other members of the recruiting committee conducted on-campus interviews for summer jobs and new associates. I concentrated on developing solid organizational and people skills during my time at this firm.

In 1990 I received a job offer to become director of recruiting on a full-time basis at the age of 26. After a year, due to the slowdown in the economy, my firm stopped hiring attorneys. I transitioned to legal marketing at the insistence and encouragement of my employer. At first, I was hesitant to take this job but my employer allowed me to take the time needed to learn legal marketing and develop a marketing philosophy for the firm. My employer stated that my skills were very strong and transferable; instead of conveying the firm's capabilities to law students and lateral attorneys, I would refocus and convey them to potential new clients.

In 1994 I was hired as the client services/marketing manager for a law firm's northern California offices. Because this firm already had an established marketing program, I was able to refine my marketing skills and implement more progressive strategies. This position was very gratifying since I worked with two very strong mentors. Two years later I received a phone call from Cooley Godward LLP, who made me a very attractive offer.

I am now the director of the client services/marketing department with 20 employees. My department members demonstrate outstanding skills in the following areas: verbal and written communications, marketing consulting and coaching, team building and facilitation, public relations and computer technology. Their projects include such items as the drafting of a biannual client letter from our managing partner, press releases, and web site management. My firm would pay a clerk who recently graduated from high school an hourly wage of $15 to 18 an hour. If the individual has no experience, but is pursuing a marketing or journalism degree, my firm would pay a salary of approximately $35,000 a year. Directors in California/New York firms can expect an income of $150,000+ a year and managers can expect an annual salary of approximately $90,000.

Four years ago, my firm had only 270 attorneys and now has approximately 700 attorneys and related support staff. For those of you who consider this growing career, I recommend that you get into it only if you like being constantly challenged—mentally and physically. Learn what the characteristics are that a specific firm wants you to have, and be realistic with yourself about being able to deliver on those expectations. Exercise good intuition and judgment—that is the key. Be able to multitask and make on-the-spot decisions regularly and confidently. Know that a job in legal marketing is fast paced, high pressure, and very exciting!

GETTING IN AND MOVING UP

Many enter this field after experience in marketing and advertising in corporate environments or after the acquisition of experience in other careers discussed in this book. Many occupations in the legal profession have job responsibilities that may provide you with experience. For example, if you work as a legal secretary, you may be responsible for maintaining a database of potential clients to whom you will mail a newsletter or holiday card. Many responsibilities that a legal marketing professional will have may also match the responsibilities of a legal administrator. You should carefully scrutinize the job responsibilities associated with a particular law firm position to determine where responsibilities may overlap with those typically associated with other careers in law.

In order to gain a position as a legal marketer you may have to work your way up through a variety of other positions discussed in this book. You should look for employment opportunities that will allow you to assume some menial, if not mundane, tasks associated with legal marketing, such as database entry and maintenance. Then you should improve your skills by taking relevant courses at a local school and work steadily toward getting an education while making the acquisition of experience your top priority. Even if you were to receive a college degree before entering this field, you would likely still have to start at an entry-level position. That is why it is so important to acquire full-time experience while getting your education part time in marketing or journalism.

If you already have law office experience, analyze your prior job responsibilities to determine what, if any, aspects of legal marketing you may have already participated in. Try to locate or create employment opportunities that will provide you with more experience in this field. You may even seek employment outside of the legal sector in a marketing or advertising firm in order to acquire some skills. The acquisition of a marketing or journalism degree can help open doors for you if you do not have the experience. If you *do* have experience and you receive a degree, you may be eligible for a higher rate of pay.

EMPLOYMENT FORECAST

As more and more of the public pursues higher education, more and more of those individuals are opting for law school. Every year the number of students entering and graduating from law school increases, which increases competition between attorneys and law firms and, therefore increases the need for legal marketing professionals. Also, law firms typically do not operate like corporations, which utilize marketers and sales techniques. In the future, more law firms will implement strategies used by corporations that will include full-time legal marketing professionals to address client needs and concerns.

Legal marketing professionals may be known by many different occupational titles with varying degrees of responsibility. Some of these other occupational titles use manager, coordinator, specialist, and director interchangeably with jobs in the following areas: marketing, client services, practice group, public relations, client development, client relations, communications, and business development.

There is a feeling among many attorneys that legal advertising is unprofessional. As a legal marketing professional, you will have to cater your recommendations and activities toward your firm's beliefs. In the future, this attitude is likely to relax, thus increasing opportunities for legal marketing professionals.

At the same time prepaid legal services are growing in popularity among the general public. This involves a client's payment of a legal insurance premium to an insurer. In exchange, the insurer contracts with attorneys to provide a variety of services at a specified rate to their customers. The attorney then receives referrals from the insurance company at the agreed-upon rate. As these programs become more popular and more attorneys participate in them, marketing efforts may be subverted by this phenomenon or redirected at legal insurance plans. However, there will always be potential clients who do not belong to a legal insurance plan, just as many people do not have medical insurance. It is unlikely that this emerging trend will decrease the need for legal marketing professionals.

EARNINGS

- On the average, marketing coordinators or directors earn between $55,000 and $80,900, and marketing coordinators earn between $35,000 and $50,000.

- Marketing coordinators or administrators with no college have a median base salary of $44,300, with some college $46,500, and with an A.A. degree $60,625.

- Marketing coordinators with no college degree earn a median of salary of $39,998 and with an A.A. degree earn $47,300.

As an entry-level legal marketing professional, your pay rate is likely to be similar to that of a legal secretary or legal assistant. The vast differences in responsibilities and duties will vary your pay rate considerably along with factors such as firm size and geographic location. Top-notch legal marketing professionals who are employed by firms can earn up to $300,000 a year. As an independent consultant, after years of experience, you can earn well in excess of this amount.

PROFESSIONAL CONNECTION

Legal Marketing Association (LMA)

401 North Michigan Avenue
Chicago, IL 60611
Tel: (312) 245-1592
Fax: (312) 321-5194
Web Site: http://www.legalmarketing.org

A FEW KEY POINTS TO REMEMBER

• There are many different levels of responsibility accorded to legal marketing professionals. Your rate of pay will vary greatly depending upon your level of responsibility.

• An education in journalism or marketing will increase opportunities for you as a legal marketing professional.

• You should have a professional image that mirrors the firm's image.

• You should be confident and poised with excellent communication skills in order to effectively deal with other attorneys and clients.

• A legal marketing professional should understand what a firm's image and ethics are.

CHAPTER SEVEN

Political Consultant

Political consultants specialize in communications with voters. Political consulting is a career that has recently come of age, alongside web-based businesses and mediation. They comprise an extremely specialized niche of marketing and advertising professionals in the limited field of government and politics.

One of the most rewarding aspects of political consulting is getting deserving candidates elected, and having an influence on society. According to Rick Carpenter, political consultant: "Nobody gets to make a law unless they are elected. If you can influence elections, you can influence society. Many times the most qualified or decent people are not masters of self-promotion. They are humble and reluctant to sing their own praises. You have to explain to that candidate that he has very few opportunities to communicate with a busy voter who has his or her own real-life problems. I have to explain to many candidates that they must tell those voters who they are and what they believe briefly and efficiently."

THE RIGHT STUFF

Political consultants should have interests in marketing and government. They should stay abreast of political issues and the effects of legislation on different groups. Relevant government issues and their effect on segments of society should be automatic knowledge.

Critical to campaigning is the incumbent's voting record. Political consultants should utilize a legislator's voting record to the campaign's benefit. This means that if the campaign is on behalf of an incumbent, the public should be told how the incumbent benefited them. If the campaign is on behalf of a challenger, the public should know about the incumbent's unpopular votes.

Political consultants use a variety of research techniques to determine what issues are of public importance and will sway voter opinions. The collection and analysis of this research is critical to the success of any campaign. Political consultants should be able to research particular constituencies and design a political plan of issues that will cater to their needs and the desires of their client.

Excellent interpersonal skills and the ability to earn trust are critical characteristics of a political consultant. Political consultants should quickly win the trust of their clients and maintain it. According to Rick Carpenter, "To clients, political consultants are often perceived as rented strangers. It is difficult for candidates to turn their lives over to a political consultant or anyone else they have just met." A political consultant must inspire trust and confidence and have excellent communication skills and political knowledge.

Political consultants should be creative and able to see issues and opportunities from every perspective. They should anticipate the opposition. Much like a chess game they have to plan actions far ahead of time and consider the long-term ramification of every move. They should know the key players in an electoral race and the legal issues and constituents in order to develop appropriate campaign strategy.

WHAT POLITICAL CONSULTANTS DO

There are many types of consultants used in a modern campaign. General consultants handle the big picture and supervise other specialized consultants who may handle direct mail, fund-raising, telemarketing, television, public speaking, and dress. Computer specialists are increasingly necessary for layout and design and information management. The number and variety of specialists that may be retained is directly related to successful fund-raising efforts.

- Political consultants develop, manage, and execute campaign plans. They spend most of their time researching political issues and constituency demographics. Then they counsel their candidates, issue interest groups, or political parties on the appropriate image to convey and issues to address. During campaign season, their lives are hectic as they continue to counsel candidates, and oversee, manage, and operate campaigns. When not in election season, they continue to counsel candidates on issues before the legislature, issue press releases, and organize fund-raisers and town hall meetings.

- Political consultants deal with the logistics of getting work product prepared and delivered to the public. For example, they develop an idea, draft it, deliver it to the graphics designer, have the product approved for printing, have it printed, then see that it gets mailed.

- Political consultants should have a constituent or fund-raiser database ready to go as well. At some point during this process, the candidate reviews and approves the product. These are the logistics of moving a product, and political consultants should be able to develop a system to ensure that the product is completed and delivered on time or their candidates will become disgruntled.

- Political consultants get involved in print advertising, which is a necessary medium to reach constituents. In every campaign, a logo must be designed to convey a candidate's image. The logo should be used in all advertising and look impressive on yard signs. Part of the campaign plan involves getting enough yard signs in place through constituent permission and volunteer efforts. The logo may also appear on buses, billboards, or newspapers.

- Political consultants conduct polls and research to determine what constituents think and want. Telemarketers are employed with an arsenal of questions to ask a particular constituency. This polling also allows candidates to know whether their campaigning efforts are being successfully implemented. There are many different ways to conduct "attitude" research of constituencies; a careful and detailed approach to drafting questions for telemarketers to ask is an integral part of any successful poll.

- Radio and television advertising may be used in certain markets if a constituency base is large enough. Political consultants should help identify appropriate messages in radio and television advertising and assist with the production and editing of these messages. Advertising spots are designed to help voters form a positive, memorable, and lasting impression of a candidate with the proper image conveyed.

- Political consultants should review the newspapers and editorial sections daily to keep abreast of what opponents are doing, public opinion, and whether press releases have been favorably covered. They should identify issues for release to the press and draft these releases with candidate approval.

- Depending on the demographics of a constituency, political consultants may recommend political web sites and on-line fund-raising. If such a recommendation is made, they will have to create the content of these sites and coordinate, direct, and approve all layout and designs. Campaign sites can include key issue information, a volunteer sign-up sheet, a candidate schedule, an issues survey and feedback form, and even receive contributions on-line.

FUND-RAISING

Fund-raising is one of the most critical aspects of a political campaign and consultants should be able to assist or direct fund-raising efforts. Specialists who earn a percentage of fees may be employed for this purpose. They should know who the key contributors are in a particular location and target those people for contributions. Without raising funds, a campaign cannot function to increase voter recognition of a candidate, and the campaign will be lost. Fund-raising efforts may be through direct mail and special fund-raising events. Direct-mail pieces and event announcements should be carefully drafted and events should be carefully planned with guest speakers present in support of a candidate.

PERSUASION MAIL

Persuasion mail is different from fund-raising mail. Fund-raising mail directly promotes campaign contributions, but persuasion mail is directed toward changing attitudes and influencing actions. Political consultants should draft text and include photographs that convey the right image. They may even oversee the photography shoot, so that the proper image is captured on film.

WHAT THE JOB IS *REALLY* LIKE

The life of political consultants during campaign season is hectic. Consultants will assist and encourage candidates on a daily basis through their ups and downs. Also, political consultants constantly supervise the designers, printers, photographers, and mail houses to ensure the timely completion of assignments consistent with the campaign schedule.

According to Rick Carpenter, political consultant: "My day begins when my earliest-rising client gets out of bed with a panic attack. This is usually about an hour before my alarm will ring. Most of my morning is taken up by a series of phone calls from candidates, printers, graphic designers, and mailing operations. These conferences are all about campaign logistics, or moving campaign materials through the various stages of production. In the afternoons, I schedule meetings, approve layouts, designs, and tear sheets, then run around to grease the squeakiest wheels.

"In the evenings, I will debrief candidates about the day's activities and discuss future strategy. After the phone calls stop, I finally have enough quiet time to draft and create campaign messages and delivery mechanisms. During an election season, I work 14 to 18 hour days and rarely sleep more than 5 to 6 hours."

At some point, a political consultant will have to make the tactical decision of whether to attack an opponent. Strategic considerations regarding whether the gain from an attack will outweigh any negative consequences by a counterattack must be made. Attacking an opponent, if done fairly and honestly, is a necessary part of the political process. Political consultants with state-level campaigns usually have to convince their candidates of this, even though an incumbent will not tell the public of his or her unpopular votes. Political consultants should refrain from false or misleading attacks on an opponent or member of his or her family. When a political consultant recommends an attack piece, it should be based on an incumbent's performance and the truth.

A Person Who's Done It

MEET RICK CARPENTER

VITAL STATISTICS

Rick Carpenter became involved in political consulting by sheer chance in 1992 when a friend of his was running for office and asked him for help. His campaign was the only successful one against an incumbent that year. Then others heard about him and began asking him to help them with their campaigns as well. Most people get started in this business by first working as a lobbyist or congressional staffer. Rick's education and employment background was in marketing and sales. This background has assisted him in his career success at the age 37, along with his genuine enjoyment of the political arena. In addition to running his own political consultant firm, he is the general consultant to his state's House Republican PAC. Here is his story.

I first knew I wanted to be a political consultant before I knew such a thing existed. I was fascinated with the campaign process, media coverage, and general excitement. I exhibited these interests before I even entered high school. During high school I would devise creative ways to get friends or myself elected to various offices, much to the chagrin of my teachers. I had always followed political issues and candidates, but never saw political consulting as a viable way to make a living. In 1992 my friend's brother decided to run for the state House and asked me to handle his campaign. That year he was the only Republican in the state to beat an incumbent Democrat!

After the election I returned to normal life, but saw the opportunity for another line of work. I went back to school and took some more political science classes with an eye toward a possible degree in the subject. I abandoned that idea after I determined that political science really had nothing to do with modern politics—my marketing education was quite sufficient. When the next election cycle came around, I had more clients and won a few more campaigns. After that, political consulting became a full-time job.

I have run about 40 campaigns over the last 8 years, mostly state legislature, city council, and county office campaigns. The primary media used has been direct mail and newspaper ads, but some television is used in certain markets.

Many people that get into campaign consulting start as staff members for local officials. Their background is in government. They learned campaign craft for a few months every other year, so they and their bosses could keep their jobs. This is changing because there is more separation between the political and government sides of an elected official's operation.

I advise others thinking about this career to learn the political process from the bottom up. My work calling or knocking on doors as a volunteer for various campaigns taught me more about voters, the decision-making process, and campaign logistics than anything else. Further, as a political consultant, you should control your emotions and maintain an outside perspective. To your client, the campaign is the most important thing in the world, but to the voters, it is a peripheral annoyance. You cannot ride the emotional roller coaster with the candidate, swinging between panic and exaltation; you have to see the campaign as the voter does. It also helps to have a slight case of attention deficit disorder, especially if you are working on several campaigns, so that you can easily handle several tasks at once.

The lucrative income in political consulting does not come in fees or retainers, but in overrides or commissions. In the 1992 Clinton campaign, James Carville, the chief political consultant, earned over $1,000,000 in commissions, but only about $200,000 from retainers. The earning potential is directly related to the cost of the market; for example, you would make more money in a New York governor's race than one in Texas because advertising in New York is so much more expensive. The key to having a healthy income is getting the advertising commission, not the monthly retainer.

Most of the money earned by political consultants is from advertising commissions. You should develop contacts with the key people you will use for this purpose. As a new political consultant you will probably work on under-funded campaigns and receive little or no pay. Otherwise, you can expect $5,000 to $10,000 per campaign with commission overrides.

GETTING IN AND MOVING UP

Starting off in this business is difficult. There are limited job opportunities for entry-level lobbyists or staff members for legislators, unless you have connections or a college degree. However, if, as an aspiring political consultant, you regularly volunteer for campaigns and are active in the political party, a job opening will likely become available to you with your newfound knowledge about the way voters think that you acquired by knocking on doors and attending functions. Through volunteer efforts, you can gain the experience needed in this profession without a college degree. Also, by staying current in technology, you may receive more opportunities.

Many political consultants are full-time employees of political parties. They are responsible for directing campaigns and for the administrative operation of their organization. Others are public affairs professionals and lobbyists who have actively contributed their time toward preferred campaigns. Still others have gotten their start by being involved in their political party or by working for a legislator. Any of these employment opportunities will help you become acclimated toward a full-time career as a political consultant.

Most decisions you will make as a political consultant involve strategic maneuvering for the benefit of your candidate. You should analyze recent elections and be familiar with strategies that did or did not work. By contacting the American Association for Political Consultants, aspiring political consultants can learn more about this profession and network opportunities and resources. There are even computer games and programs such as Doonesbury Election game that can help political consultants hone in on strategic skills.

An education in journalism, English, literature, or marketing will be helpful as well. In order to move up in this field, you should develop a writing style that appeals to the layperson, and is direct and powerfully persuasive. You should know how to create messages and deliver them effectively to a variety of constituencies. Some universities and junior colleges have classes available that will help in these areas.

As a point of information, few universities other than George Washington University in Washington, D.C., offer degrees in political consulting. Rick Carpenter says, "You need to be able to apply a broad base of knowledge to the electoral process. Use what you know and be willing to learn and adapt. Most political consultants are well educated in several fields. In the end you have to get people elected to office. Once you do, nobody asks what your major was in college."

EMPLOYMENT FORECAST

There are more than 500,000 elections per year with anywhere from one to six candidates vying for the positions. This means that there are on the average 1,500,000 possible clients for political consultants annually. The recognition of political consulting as a career is growing even though it has been a profession throughout our history. More than a billion dollars is spent each year on campaign advertising. Indeed, this business is growing rapidly as political consultants organize.

A growing number of corporations and other public interest groups interested in public policy are hiring political consultants as members of their public relations and public affairs departments. Political consultants are a very specialized niche of marketing and public relations professionals. Their perceived value to companies and candidates is increasing every year.

As democracy expands and more and more foreign governments adopt political processes similar to our own, U.S. political consultants are entering the international market for candidates. With democracy spreading around the globe, so are professional politics. Some say Gary Nordlinger, the former Executive Officer of the American Association of Political Consultants, now has a bigger reputation south of the border than he does in the United States.

EARNINGS

The income potential for political consultants is lucrative. Top consultants in a presidential race earn millions. Senate races earn consultants about $1,000,000 and U.S. congressional races are worth about $1–200,000, depending on the size of the state or district. Political consultants can easily command $10,000 to $20,000 a month.

In the beginning, you will probably have to do volunteer work without pay to learn the process and network with other politically minded people. You must build a reputation and acquire clients before you can earn any income. After five years, you should average at least three campaigns per election cycle, if not more, and earn $5,000 to $10,000 per campaign with commissions on advertising in excess of this. Your income will vary dramatically, depending on whether you are able to generate clients and what commission you negotiate with advertising service providers.

PROFESSIONAL CONNECTIONS

American Association of Political Consultants (AAPC)

600 Pennsylvania Avenue, SE

Suite 330

Washington, DC 20003

Tel: (202) 544-9815

Fax: (202) 544-9816

E-mail: *aacpmail@aol.com*

Web Site: *http://www.theaapc.org*

International Association of Political Consultants (IAPC)

Ken Feltman, Vice-President IAPC

927 15th Street, NW, Suite 1000

Washington, DC 20005

Tel: (202) 659-4300

Fax: (202) 371-1467

Web Site: *http://www.iapc.org*

A FEW KEY POINTS TO REMEMBER

• Before working as a political consultant, you should volunteer to work on campaigns and network with others in order to learn how the process works. You will probably have to do this before landing employment, unless you know someone or have extensive education.

• You should work as a staff member for an elected official, issue interest group, or political party before assuming the financial risk of political consulting, especially if you plan to work independently.

• Make sure you keep abreast of new technology available for campaigns and continue education efforts through membership in organizations such as the American Association of Political Consultants.

• Many career opportunities exist working for issue interest groups.

• More and more political consultants are entering the international market for candidates.

CHAPTER EIGHT

Court Reporter

After acquiring the requisite training at a junior college or vocational school, and typing speed using machine shorthand, anyone can acquire a state certification in court reporting. With this certification, you can have a rewarding career in free-lance or official reporting, making more money than many college graduates. Although court reporting requires hard work, concentration, familiarity with new technology, and attention to detail, it is also exciting to be a critical player in litigation. Of all the careers in law without the need for a college degree, court reporting usually involves the most face-to-face contact with the people and witnesses who are the subject of suits.

THE RIGHT STUFF

Court reporters should have communication and computer skills as well as the requisite training and state and national certifications. They should have above-average English-language skills and a knowledge of legal, medical, engineering, business, and medical terminology. The technological applications of court reporting and litigation support software require knowledge of computer operations. Through training at a vocational school or junior college, court reporters learn how to operate their equipment, and type at least 175 words of dictation per minute, preferably in excess of 225 words. A high school diploma may also be required. State certification and national certification requirements of the National Court Reporters Association must be met for most employment. Other personal characteristics that will ensure success as a court reporter are an ability to be well organized and to work hard, attention to detail, and effective communications with people.

WHAT COURT REPORTERS DO

- Using machine shorthand, court reporters record testimony taken in depositions and at other official proceedings. These recordings are accurate, word-for-word records, and are made most commonly with computerized stenotype machines. Records are also made in written shorthand or with video cameras. Regardless of the type of recording used, an audiotape recorder is generally a backup of the proceeding. Reporters don't have to work strictly in courtrooms. Graduates have gone to closed-captioned TV transcription work or freelance work.

- Court reporters must acquire training in the use of machine shorthand, in order to reach typing speeds of 225 words per minute. Machine shorthand involves the use of a very small keyboard, with the keys of the machine encoded to represent syllables, words, and even entire phrases. Because there are fewer keys involved, it is possible to type much faster.

- Although deposition testimony is most common among freelance court reporters, other forms of testimony are also taken by official court reporters for the government, including trials and other hearings. Many types of court proceedings may be transcribed, if requested by an attorney. This includes trials comprised of direct and cross-examinations, opening and closing statements, judicial opinions, jury instructions, and the judgment or sentence by the court. Any hearing before a judge may be transcribed. Generally, attorneys request a court reporter when they want to preserve the record for an appeal relating to any matter that comes before the Court.

• Court reporters also perform other functions besides just transcribing proceedings or testimony. They may be asked to read portions of the transcript during a deposition or trial, or may have to ask speakers to clarify inaudible statements or provide the proper spelling of names.

• Machine shorthand is not always used. Court reporters also take notes of proceedings by shorthand or other stenographic means. They may type recorded telephone conversations or other materials or dictate material into recording machines.

WHAT THE JOB IS *REALLY* LIKE

As a court reporter, you should arrive at least 30 minutes prior to any proceeding you transcribe. You must make sure to be well rested and fed before beginning your job as many attorneys prefer to work through breaks and lunch, leaving the court reporter without personal breaks. You must swear in all witnesses and confirm that the usual stipulations between the parties, the case style, if a trial date is set, and whether or not the deposition was taken pursuant to agreement or subpoena.

You should take care to transcribe every word spoken in case you are asked to read a prior question or testimony. You should also take care to get the correct spelling of names and ask witnesses who are inaudible to repeat themselves, only if necessary. Many times, two people will speak at once, inadvertently or in the heat of an argument that could border on a brawl. You should not stop transcribing at any time unless each opposing counsel agrees to go off the record. The examination of witnesses could take all day, and could even go into the evening if all the parties agree to extend the hours beyond 5:00 P.M. At the end of the testimony, witnesses should be asked whether they want to read and sign the original or waive that right. If this right is waived, the original will stand without the deponent being given a chance to proofread his or her answers. If not, the witness will be asked to review the transcript and sign a jurat page and errata sheet that indicate their changes and approval of the testimony.

After the transcribing is complete, you should prepare the transcript and all other options requested by an attorney. This may be done at the office or in the convenience of your own home, depending on your job. Scrupulous attention to detail is required by proofreaders of the transcript. If an attorney requests a rush job, you may have to work all night in order to finalize the transcript. You may need to prepare a condensed transcript that usually has four pages, or an index that refers to the location of terms by line and page number. Time stamping will allow you to synchronize transcripts with video-recorded testimony. An ASCII disk provides attorneys with an electronic transcript to be downloaded into their litigation support software. After the transcript and all final options are prepared, you are ready to make copies and bind the transcripts before mailing them out.

If a deponent has chosen to read and sign, you should provide them with a jurat page and errata sheet that generally should be returned to them within 30 days and included with the original.

A Person Who's Done It

MEET KELLY BRYANT

VITAL STATISTICS

Kelly Bryant started her career when she was 19 years old. She has worked as an administrative assistant, office manager, freelance reporter, and court reporting firm owner in her approximately 13 years in the court reporting profession. Kelly has just turned 32 and already has her own successful small business as the owner of her own court reporting firm, making a sizeable income that is much higher than most college graduates her age.

Kelly is a prime example of what the truly ambitious and motivated person can do in this lucrative field. With her lively and extroverted personality, it is no wonder that Kelly can generate so many clients for her business. However, although this skill helps her achieve success, she is also hard working and pays considerable attention to detail. Here is her story.

My father was 26 when he decided to become a court reporter; I was then only 3 years old. I always admired and respected my father. He worked his way through court reporting school as a painter. I grew up around transcripts, and hearing discussions about exciting cases and depositions. I even helped my father with his work on occasion. Even though my father earned only $200 a week as a painter when he worked his way through court-reporting school, he still managed to support his family with my mother's help.

I always knew I wanted to be a court reporter, even though after high school I briefly explored other options. While in high school, I began studying court reporting, and the foreign language of court reporters that I had to learn. I worked as an aerobics instructor at this time. Because my father wanted me to go to college, I spent one year at Texas Tech where I worked part time as a security guard in a booth at the campus gates. After one year of college, I called it quits.

In 1986 I began my schooling for court reporting in a junior college. However, summer classes were not offered, which made it difficult for me to increase my speed with such long breaks. Eventually, I transferred to a private college that offered a two-year court reporting degree year-round. After two years of study and practice, I earned my court reporter degree.

I first became exposed to professional employment in the court reporting field when I took a job working in the back room of a Dallas court reporting firm. I was responsible for binding and copying transcripts, preparing original transcripts, and billing. In order to increase my income and experience, I began working after hours at a law firm typing pleadings for $7 an hour. Eventually, my court reporting firm promoted me to office manager, which involved confirming depositions and scheduling reporters.

I passed the Arkansas and National Certification tests while at the court reporting firm and was able to take a few freelance assignments to gain experience while still in court reporting school. When I passed my state certification requirements and I began to look for employment with a firm that I could purchase after I acquired more experience. After interviewing with several prominent firms, I decided to accept employment with a near retirement-age reporter who offered to sell her practice at the end of three years. This allowed me to get the experience I needed while developing relationships with existing clients and new ones, and developing legal ties in the community. Three years later, in 1996, I bought my employer's business for the purchase price of one year of accounts receivables. Then I bought the accounts of another court reporter as well. The transition went smoothly and I was introduced to the bigger clients to ease the transition and contribute to my success.

I believe that effective court reporters should be flexible, organized, customer-oriented, and friendly. They should be willing to work long hours and occasionally have vacations cancelled. I have five to six court reporters in my employ on an independent contractor basis in the Midwest. They keep busy and earn an average income of $40,000 a year.

A typical day for these employees could involve a day at home transcribing or actual appearances at proceedings. The court reporters are to be on call at all times and be able to put in the work hours that are necessary if an attorney requests a rushed project. While on standby, court reporters transcribe prior depositions. Scopists and proofreaders are needed to verify the accuracy of transcripts. Scopists perform computerized editing from the transcripts of a court reporter. Court reporter should be able to balance their workload and personal life because one can easily run into the other. Generally, they enjoy more flexibility in their work hours compared to other jobs, but if an attorney requests that a project be rushed, the reporter has to be willing to pull an all-nighter or do whatever it takes to complete the project on time.

Court reporters in my firm make up to $80,000 a year depending on how hard they are willing to work.

GETTING IN AND MOVING UP

If you want to be a court reporter you must gain admittance to and complete the requirements of a vocational school or two-year college in court reporting. The quicker you increase your typing speed, the sooner you can graduate. Once you have completed this training you must pass the certification requirements promulgated by the state in which you live. It is also beneficial to your employment potential to gain certification from the National Court Reporters Association.

Employers will expect you to be well dressed—conservatively, of course—punctual, and proficient in your transcribing and proofreading. If an attorney wants a job rushed, you should be able to complete the job within whatever time parameters are designated. Official court reporters work eight-to-five shifts with extra time sometimes required for transcribing in the evenings.

EMPLOYMENT FORECAST

In 1996 courts nationwide employed more than 50,000 reporters, according to the U.S. Bureau of Labor Statistics. Although budget cuts may limit the ability of courts to hire more court reporters, even when court dockets are overloaded, demand should increase for court reporters willing to take depositions for court reporting service bureaus or those willing to freelance, like those reporters who work for Kelly Bryant.

Some believe that computer and voice recognition technology will replace court reporters. This is unlikely in the near future because they are always needed to read back courtroom and deposition testimony, and fill in testimony gaps when information is lost. Also, voice recognition technology cannot decipher the words of unfamiliar speakers. Eventually, this technology may be used to edit transcripts; however, it is unlikely that this technology will replace court reporters at any time in the near future.

EARNINGS

Although earnings vary with education, experience, and geographic location, court reporters generally earn a good salary with a nationwide median compensation of $45,000 a year and an average income of $50,000 a year. Nationally, court reporters earn between $18,500 and $60,000 a year, according to the Federal Labor Statistics Bureau. Generally, their income will depend upon what part of the country they live in and how much they work.

Official courtroom reporters generally earn a salary and benefits plus some compensation per page, regulated by law in most jurisdictions. Freelance reporters usually earn all or most of their income from transcripts of depositions and other out-of-court proceedings, charging what the market will bear; thus, income depends on the number of pages transcribed at rates that vary with the circumstances. Court reporters earn more on rush jobs and the number of attorneys who order transcripts can increase rates.

PROFESSIONAL CONNECTION

Contact the proper authorities in the state in which you wish to work to find out about the requirements for court reporting applicable to you. Local colleges and vocational schools that offer court reporting degrees may also be of help. In addition to your local court reporters' association, begin by contacting:

National Court Reporters Association (NCRA)
8224 Old Courthouse Road
Vienna, VA 22182
Tel: (800) 272-6272
Fax: (703) 556-6291
E-mail: *msic@ncrahq.org*
Web Site: *http://www.verbatimreporters.com*

A FEW KEY POINTS TO REMEMBER

- The harder you work, the higher your income will be.
- You may be able to acquire a temporary certification in your state to begin working before you receive your state certification.
- The faster you type, with the fewest errors, the more opportunities will be available to you.
- Certification from the National Court Reporters Association will greatly increase your marketability.
- An ability to handle difficult lawyers amicably, attention to detail, and an ability to complete tasks on time are critical.
- Court reporters earn more on rush jobs and according to the number of attorneys who order transcripts.

CHAPTER NINE

Private Investigator

P rivate investigators are commonly known as detectives. They learn how to use public databases and other resources to investigate people or entities. Many private investigators work directly with clients or are hired by attorneys. Private investigators and attorneys often perform similar investigative work, but if surveillance or undercover work is needed, attorneys usually prefer not to do such work themselves, but opt a licensed private investigator.

According to one private investigator with his own agency, Gary Moore of Accurate Investigations, he receives a great deal of satisfaction in divorce and custody matters when his work helps a client obtain a settlement for custody. This saves his clients $10,000 to $20,000 in attorney fees and costs, and up to two years of litigation. He usually does this by acquiring evidence of soon-to-be divorced people in possibly compromising situations. Although generally, as a matter of law, this is not dispositive of the custody dispute in many states, it can convince a party to give the other custody without protracted litigation.

Overall, he says, if a private investigator "solves the puzzle, he solves the problem."

THE RIGHT STUFF

Private investigators learn the skills they need through experience and generally not in any academic institution, so degrees are relatively unimportant to success as a private investigator. An investigator should be mature, able to work alone, think logically, react quickly, exercise sound judgment, and keep a professional distance from work. A solo private investigator should have the skills required to make any small business successful, including solid budgeting, client-relations skills, a strong work ethic, and an independent style. Private investigators in larger agencies must be skilled at prioritizing, writing reports, using a variety of institutionalized resources, and working with teams of other detectives.

To be a private investigator you should have street sense, analytical abilities, and curiosity. You should be detailed, diligent, and thorough. Your communication and other social skills should be excellent so that you can listen, put others at ease, put on an act if needed, and understand body language to assess credibility. You should be able to maintain professional distance, tolerate stress, and persevere. Private investigators should be confident and knowledgable about many areas of life, but tolerant and non-judgmental at the same time. They should be in excellent physical condition and health with a calm and steady temperament. Operational knowledge of photography and videography is helpful during surveillance and undercover operations.

As a private investigator, you should be able to effectively deal with legal professionals and their demands, even if difficult and tenuous at times. You will have to perform many tasks routinely assigned to attorneys, learn how to investigate a person, and develop valuable investigative contacts. Involvement with legal issues and lawyers is one of the most prominent features of a private investigator's daily life.

WHAT PRIVATE INVESTIGATORS DO

- Private investigators investigate people, businesses or entities, incidents, accidents, or crimes.

- They may be hired to interview witnesses, serve subpoenas, inspect, photograph or video people, places, or things, or coordinate activities with expert witnesses. They may even evaluate arrests and police procedures.

- A great deal of work exists for private investigators in the area of insurance fraud, particularly for Workers' Compensation and life or health insurance programs.

- Private investigators verify the activities of people who are soon to be divorced, and confirm details that may affect alimony and custody determinations or as otherwise directed.

- Private investigators can confirm a stalker's malicious attempts to harass others, so that stalking claims have increased credibility.

- Businesses may hire private investigators to work undercover for them to disclose employee theft, drug abuse at work, and protection of trade secrets, patents, and copyrights. They may conduct background checks on the financial stability of a company or prospective business partner. They report information obtained through interviews, background investigation, and surveillance, to their clients regarding
  1. the character, reputation, credibility, trustworthiness, honesty, integrity, identity, habits, conduct, business, occupation, knowledge, efficiency, loyalty, activity, movement, whereabouts, affiliations, associations, transactions, or acts of any person.
  2. crimes or wrongs committed.
  3. the cause for libels, losses, accidents, damages, injuries to persons or to property, or fires.

4. the securing of evidence.

5. the location, recovery, or disposition of lost or stolen property.

Initially, private investigators should conduct in-depth interviews with clients regarding the investigated person's habits, activities, and schedule. They should utilize this information as much as possible during their work. They may request a photograph; home and work contact information; date of birth; driver's license and social security numbers; and make, model, year, and tag of an automobile, along with a list of addresses for friends, family, acquaintances, and frequently visited establishments. The more facts private investigators learn from the client, the more likely they will be able to anticipate the activities of an individual, especially if surveillance is requested.

An investigator may search electronic or other on-site databases for information regarding a subject. Most private investigators subscribe to various expensive on-line services that they use to locate people and perform credit and other background checks. Some sites that contain a multitude of links to informational databases that are free or require the payment of a fee include

State Public Records Online, Free	*http://www.pimall.com/nais/ statedb.html*
The National Association of Investigative Specialists, Inc.	*http://www.pimall.com/nais/ links.html*
Information Brokers Inside the PI Mall	*http://www.pimall.com/name/ brokers.html*

Private investigators frequently search court records for prior workers' compensation claims, criminal charges and convictions, marriage information, and litigation history. Many court dockets are now available on-line and anyone can search by party name for litigation and criminal charge history. Although many free Internet resources are available, they may be not be current enough for an investigator's needs. However, because so many public record databases are on-line, many private investigators utilize these resources on a continuing basis for basic background information. Here are some of the best sites for general information regarding subjects.

ACCU-Source	http://www.accu-source.com/
Advanced Research inc.	http://www.advsearch.com
Atlas Information Services	http://www.pimall.com
ATT Information Services	http://members.icanect.net/~att/
Daily Planet Information Services	http://www.pimall.com/dailyplanet/index.html
IRSC	http://www.irsc.com
CDB Infotec	http://www.cdb.com/public/
Confi-Check	http://www.Confi-chek.com/
Knowx	http://www.knowx.com/
Masterfacts	http://www.masterfacts.com/
Megasource	http://www.megasource.com/
National Credit Information	http://www.pimall.com/nci
Merlin Information Services	http://www.merlindata.com
Dig Dirt	http://www.pimall.com/digdirt/index.html
Wind Associates	http://www.windsearch.com/
Track'Em	http://www.toolcity.net/~richreen/trackem.html
Tredi-Info Services	http://cust.iamerica.net/rediinfo
Vital Records on the Internet	http://vitalrec.com/index.html

Before conducting any surveillance, private investigators should discover whatever they can about an individual's prior criminal, financial, marital, employment, residence, credit, and other histories. Private investigators may also review tax filings, recorded deeds, news reports, and other periodicals, depending on the purpose of their investigation. Private investigators investigate subjects or locate missing persons through their comprehensive review of electronic databases to which they subscribe, as well as the Internet and by searching court records. They also have confidential contacts and conduct personal interviews to acquire information.

"DUMPSTER DIVING"

Prior to the formulation of efficient surveillance recommendations, many private investigators engage in "dumpster diving," which involves picking up trash placed in a designated area for public disposal. With latex-gloved hands and rubber boots, private investigators sift through a subject's trash to learn about the habits of an individual, as well as to acquire any incriminating or otherwise enlightening materials. In many states, once a subject places trash on the curb for public disposal, the subject can no longer claim a privacy interest in the garbage. However, state laws vary and the investigator should research and comply with these laws according to the law in a given area.

SURVEILLANCE ACTIVITIES

Private investigators should attempt to coordinate surveillance activities with the best estimated optimal times to catch the subject in compromising activities. After conducting all interviews and background investigation, and performing dumpster diving, private investigators should have developed a plan of surveillance at the most optimal and cost-efficient manner. Breaking up surveillance sessions is usually the best way to provide a client with maximum coverage.

Much surveillance work is tedious and boring as investigators wait and watch on foot, in a building, or generally, in a vehicle, for hours on end. Many times, private investigators should use other investigators to assist with proper surveillance, but cannot due to limited client funds for such services. However, many investigators, such as Gary Moore, employ others to help with tailing because of the big risk of "blowing one's cover or losing a subject." During surveillance, investigators are subject to the whims and caprices of individuals and must react accordingly.

One of the most exhilarating aspects of surveillance involves "tailing" individuals on foot or by car. This requires an investigator to be in tune with the behavior of the individual and the crowd. Gary Moore says, "This does not involve an action-packed car chase or an investigator's cover will be blown." Private investigators generally use two or more shield cars, depending on the density of traffic. Tailing individuals is generally the most difficult of investigative skills to master. Many private investigators use nondescript vehicles with two-way radios and a series of disguises to avoid recognition.

- Fixed surveillance activities require private investigators to remain at a fixed location from the best possible shielded vantage point. Private investigators sometimes covertly hide in the backseat of a car or van so that it appears no one is in the car. Other times, they may pretend their vehicle is broken down and they await the arrival of the automobile club to help.

- Loose fixed surveillance is required when a fixed vehicle would cause too much attention. This requires sporadic checks by two vehicles to decrease suspicion that might be present with one vehicle.

- Private investigators may pretend to be telephone repair people, power company employees, street repair people, traffic counters, and road surveyors, as long as they dress the part with the attendant tools, and acquire appropriate permission. After all, no one is likely to question a private investigator who dangles from a telephone pole and appears to be fixing a line!

- Finally, private investigators may be hired to perform undercover work and assume an identity to get direct answers from an individual that cannot be obtained by any other means. Undercover work is generally designed to discover deviant activities, watch people without arousing their suspicions, perform security checks, and assess loyalty and character. Private investigators who perform undercover work must be able to act and learn their roles and appropriate jargon to fit within a group. Gary Moore has worked undercover in bars and clubs, department stores, and in companies. Undercover investigations may be conducted regarding workplace issues, shoplifting and other crimes, and the social and neighborhood activities of individuals. Undercover work tends to be the most exhilarating and stressful of all an investigator's responsibilities.

REPORTS

Investigators should create written reports upon client demand and payment. These reports measure the standard, quality, and professionalism of an investigator's performance. A well-written report should paint a factual picture of a person or incident, contain factual information that will influence a reader, and guide a client toward further action without bias or embellishment. They should be concise, factual and informative, clear, chronological, complete, accurate, and objective. Profiles of interviewees should include a physical description of gender, ethnicity, hair color, eye color, age, height, and weight. Additional standards exist for the descriptions of vehicles and other property in written reports.

When preparing a written report, private investigators should review their notes and prepare an outline of their activities along with the results. The report should be drafted with reference to specific times, dates, and quantities; reports that are concrete rather than abstract are the preferred style of investigative reports. For example, instead of writing, "A few days ago in the afternoon, we found a large quantity of stolen items," a private investigator should write, "On August 23, 2000 at 2:30 P.M., John Henry and I found nine stolen vehicles at the suspect's residence." Reports are best prepared when drafted as a work-in-progress during the course of an investigation. At the conclusion of the investigation a final report may be more expeditiously prepared and submitted.

Without consent, private investigators may not divulge investigative information to anyone other than his client. Private investigators may not willfully make a false statement or report to a client, employer, or authorized representative concerning information acquired.

WHAT THE JOB IS *REALLY* LIKE

Some say the life of a private investigator is mostly confined to background checks and finding lost people. Others say they mostly do surveillance work with long, monotonous, and tedious hours of sitting and waiting. Overall, 40 percent of a general private investigator's work involves divorce and custody battles, but as a private investigator you may have other clients. For example, you may have annual contracts with corporations to investigate internal problems and protect trade secrets.

For the first two years of employment at an investigative agency, a great deal of research is performed. If you start your own agency, you may expect to battle all the problems of a small-business owner, such as generating clients, fluctuating income, and unpredictable staffing needs. After about five years, many agencies add security services to increase their clientele. After ten years, private investigators employed by firms should supervise others or look toward starting their own agency. The majority of private investigators who leave the profession do so between four and eight years, if they have not started their own agencies.

Gary Moore says his days vary weekly and tend to go in cycles, sometimes depending on the season. During holidays such as Christmas, he receives numerous calls on domestic issues. "Every morning, I answer phone calls from prospective clients starting at about 7:30 A.M. Many of these people simply need someone to talk to and I act as counselor when they call. Some of these calls result in clients and some do not. It's all part of the job. I must spend mornings with my mother who is in need of medical care, but I am able to take calls at this time. I place my office phone on call forward when I am not there. In the afternoons, I am generally in my office and conduct research by placing search requests with libraries and handling other administrative matters. I perform some of my research once a week at a public library. Surveillance tends to be cyclical and I average around two to three weeks on surveillance and the same amount of time off. Surveillance work is generally boring and tedious."

A Person Who's Done It

MEET GARY MOORE

VITAL STATISTICS

Gary Moore has worked as a licensed contract private investigator for the past 30 years. When he began his private investigation company, he worked at it for about five years while working in another business he had, until he became disenchanted with his profession. So he returned to his horse and cattle business until he was called back into the investigative field to investigate animal cruelty. After many investigative successes and personal satisfaction from his animal cruelty investigations, he has been active in his profession for the past 20 years. Here is his story.

In 1967 I had previously been in the military and worked for the United States Post Office. With my own horseshoeing business as a backup, I decided to start working as a private investigator. I became disenchanted doing divorce and custody, and left the profession for about five years when I had twice located a client's soon-to-be-ex-wife with the support of the client's counsel who stated he needed to serve her papers. Unfortunately, both times the client discovered his wife's whereabouts, he beat her up. From this experience, I learned to always make sure I am comfortable with the client's purpose for the investigation. If clients do not appear to be on the up-and-up, then I do not accept them as clients. When I returned to the profession, I found a cause that interested me—animal cruelty. I investigated animal cruelty cases and catered to more corporate clients. Only 25 percent of my cases now involve divorce, but they do not bother me as they did in the beginning, and I am much more careful about the clients I help.

In 1988 the laws began to regulate private investigators more, and private investigators had to qualify for their profession unless they had previously worked in law enforcement. Many private investigators are retired from law enforcement. Out of approximately 100 investigators located in my community, only about six appear to pursue their careers full time and 50 percent are retired from other jobs. This may explain why average incomes are not higher.

There are some dishonest private investigators out there, as there are in other professions, so people should be careful about who they hire. If you are a full-time private investigator who treats his clients ethically, you can earn anywhere from $15,000 to $30,000 a year in the Midwest. Private investigators in the Midwest and South charge anywhere from $45 to $75 an hour. In major cities, investigators charge as much as $100 an hour. I generate my clients from referrals, Yellow Pages advertising, legal journals and periodicals, and other advertising. Word-of-mouth referrals can be hard to get when dealing with the general public because many people are reluctant to admit they hired a private investigator.

I advise anyone interested in entering this profession to have another income, especially if they are just starting out. A new investigator should start out as an apprentice in an agency to learn the ropes. Investigators should have patience and communication skills to deal with frustrated clients. They should be sure they are in compliance with all state and local rules regarding their profession and state licensing requirements.

GETTING IN AND MOVING UP

At larger investigative firms a degree in criminal behavior, psychology, or law enforcement may be a plus, but these firms will likely primarily consider your temperament and prior experience. About 75 percent of private investigators have a law enforcement, security, or military background. Some private investigators attend private detective schools.

With the increase in demand for legal services will come an increase in demand for private investigators. Many private investigators are fly-by-night part-timers and do not do a thorough job or provide their clients with detailed reports. There is a definite shortage of stable private investigative firms that are able to comprehensively address client needs in a cost-efficient fashion.

If you are interested in this profession, the most effective way to get into it is to meet your state requirements for licensure and work with a larger private investigation firm for as much time as you need to learn the ropes. While working in such capacities, you should begin to format a business plan for an agency and purchase some of the equipment you will need, which includes a 35 mm camera, video camera, night vision glasses and lens, binoculars, computer with software, desk, and scanner to pick up radio frequencies.

Most states have boards of private investigators that regulate the profession and require private investigators to obtain a license. The state boards usually establish training programs to be conducted by approved institutions for the acquisition of a license. Annual renewal training may be required. In order to become a private investigator, one is likely to have to pass an examination, have some education and/or training, and post a bond. If you are considering a career in investigative work, you should contact the authorities in your area for more information. Training programs usually address legal limitations on the use of firearms and on the powers and authority of the private investigator. State laws applicable to their services will be reviewed along with field note taking and report writing, range firing, and handgun safety and maintenance.

Many private investigators belong to the newsgroup alt.private.investigator with The PI Mall at *http://www.pimall.com/private-eye/index.html*. This is a great resource for information and networking in the field of private investigating.

Private investigative agencies are expected to grow rapidly and increase in size over the next 10 to 15 years, as is the field of law. Economies of scale make it likely that larger, more technologically advanced firms will begin to consolidate many of the smaller firms. This will likely increase the average income for new private investigators and create a generous cash flow for the owners of such firms. If you begin the process of becoming a private investigator and learn how to operate your own business now, you can be the owner of one of these technologically advanced firms at the right time.

EMPLOYMENT FORECAST

As technology increases, more and more people will be able to access information that was once within the almost exclusive domain and expertise of the private investigator. However, the field of private investigation is still expected to grow by 15,000 jobs per year in the 10-year period from 1998 to 2008, with a total of 76,000 jobs expected. While the *new* jobs will average about 15,000 a year over that period, the unemployment rate for investigators will still be very high. The uncertainty of the work, with long hours and uneven pay, is the most significant reason people leave the profession. If you have the desire to start your own business and have the aptitude and personal characteristics required to do so, you will be able to find clients. Also, private investigators do more than just investigate people. They may work in security, as undercover agents, accident reconstruction experts, or alarm systems agents.

EARNINGS

Private investigators have an average starting salary of $16,500. After five years the average income increases to $27,500, and after 10 to 15 years their average salary is $40,000. These figures may be low due to the high number of part-time investigators. Private investigators can earn well in excess of these figures if they have a keen business sense and build up their own agencies.

PROFESSIONAL CONNECTIONS

Most states have their own association of private investigators; contact the one near you for more information. There are also the following national associations that can assist you.

National Association of Investigative Specialists, Inc.
P.O. Box 33244
Austin, TX 78764
Tel: (512) 719-3595
Fax: (512) 719-3594
E-mail: rthomasoon@aol.com
Web Site: http://www.pimall.com/nais/links.html

National Association of Legal Investigators
6109 Meadowwood
Grand Blanc, MI 48439
Tel: (800) 266-6254
Fax: (810) 694-7109
E-Mail: *lacardo@gfn*
Web Site: *http://www.nationline.org*

Society of Professional Investigators
80 8th Avenue, Suite 303
New York, NY 10011
Tel: (212) 625-3533
(718) 331-7400
Fax: (718) 259-2550
E-mail: admin@spionline.org
Web Site: http://www.spionline.org

World Association of Detectives
P.O. Box 441470-301
Aurora, CO 80044
Tel: (800) 962-0516
Fax: (303) 671-6063
E-mail: wadinc@uswest.net

A FEW KEY POINTS TO REMEMBER

- You must meet your particular state's requirements for licensure before working as a private investigator.
- In order to generate a higher income than average, you will have to have keen business sense and the ability and daring to start your own agency.
- Prior experience in law enforcement, in security, or in the military may be helpful, but is not required.
- You should exhibit professionalism and generate detailed reports for clients regarding your services and activities.

CHAPTER TEN

Deputy Court Clerk

I f you have ever seen a deputy court clerk in action you have mostly heard, "stamp, stamp, stamp, stamp, stamp!" Deputy court clerks are experts on pleadings and filing procedures. Many times an attorney will call a court clerk for advice on how to file a document because of the clerk's expertise. Deputy court clerks are not supposed to give such advice to the general public because to do so could constitute the unauthorized practice of law. They gain invaluable expertise regarding filing requirements, setting hearings, investigation of archived cases, and general know-how regarding courthouse operation and procedure.

THE RIGHT STUFF

Experience as a deputy court clerk is most valuable, even though the work is paper-intensive. Deputy court clerks perform work similar to that of a legal secretary, legal administrator, and legal secretary. They must have excellent organizational skills with paperwork and file maintenance, and should be able to repeat similar tasks. They should be computer proficient with some writing skills and must develop a high wrist-to-finger speed to process paperwork. Although continuing education could be beneficial, it is not required in order to work as a deputy court clerk and move through the hierarchical rank of clerks. Deputy court clerks must be able to effectively deal with the general public through active listening skills and dealing with angry or unpleasant people in conflict situations. They should also know the statutory requirements of their positions.

WHAT DEPUTY COURT CLERKS DO

- A deputy court clerk supports the court clerk's administrative functions to ensure the efficient operation of the court as prescribed by statute.

- Deputy court clerks work in different divisions of a courthouse such as civil, criminal, traffic, probate, juvenile and deprived children, protective orders, front offices, small claims, domestic, licensing, cost administration and budgeting, accounting, microfilm, records and archives, as well as others. Tasks and informational knowledge required as a deputy court clerk vary to some extent, depending on which division a court clerk is assigned to.

- Some deputy court clerks double as "floaters" to assist judges when their support staff is unavailable. The main responsibilities of deputy court clerks include communicating with the public and attorneys regarding filing requirements, and ensuring that all documents presented in person, via fax, or through the mail are file stamped. They must then file, organize, and maintain all case records and enter data into the computer systems. Deputy court clerks may also research cases to provide information to the public and maintain receipts and other accounting ledgers.

RECORDS

Records that are kept by deputy court clerks may include case files, receipts, appearance dockets and indexes, general indexes, journal records, motion, hearing, disposition and trial dockets, juror attendance, claims and fee records, search warrants, and child support registries. They may certify and authenticate court documents. Deputy court clerks make sure the public has access to all records, except those under protective seal or specifically excluded from the public domain by statute. Records that are typically not subject to disclosure are those on adoption, juvenile and children cases, mental health cases, guardianship cases, and wills filed for safekeeping. Deputy court clerks may prepare reports regarding general statistical information, bail bonds, licensing to tax commissions, unclaimed property, dispute resolutions, convictions, law library, indigent defense, D.U.I., and court funds, as well as others.

WHAT THE JOB IS *REALLY* LIKE

Deputy court clerks generally work a standard business day and 40-hour workweek with one-hour lunch breaks. Their workdays are hectic and require excellent organizational skills to handle the paperwork. Sally Howe-Smith, Court Clerk of the District Court of Tulsa County, says deputy court clerks typically "wait on people at the various counters, answer telephone inquiries, file documents into court files and open cases, enter data on parties and cases, and take and receipt monies paid to the court." Her typical day involves, "answering phone calls, assisting department heads with problems, interviewing prospective employees, working on computer problems, and signing necessary documents." Once a deputy court clerk becomes the head of a department, his or her typical day includes supervision of employees and ensuring their adequate performance, and taking problem calls.

A Person Who's Done It

MEET SALLY HOWE-SMITH

VITAL STATISTICS

Sally Howe-Smith has worked as a deputy court clerk for approximately 21 years and as the district court clerk for 10 years. She was elected to her current position. She is professionally affiliated with many local associations. She is a guest speaker at numerous schools and civic organizations regarding the court clerk's office, how to conduct records research, small claims court procedures, and other topics of general interest. Before becoming the court clerk, she had positions throughout the deputy court clerk hierarchy, ranging from entry-level deputy court clerk to second deputy court clerk, when she engaged in a variety of duties including hiring, training, and evaluating the performance of deputy court clerks, to chief deputy court clerk, when she assisted the court clerk with many of the functions she now performs. Here is her story.

I began working in the traffic division of the Tulsa County Courthouse during the summers of 1971 and 1972. I then became a full-time floating minute clerk, responsible for assisting judges when their staff was unavailable, by recording minute orders. After only two years of full-time experience, I was promoted to department head of the Traffic Division and of the Domestic and License Division, with supervisory responsibility over a staff of 12. I ran for election for Court Clerk in 1993 and won. Now I have a multitude of functions to perform that help the 119 deputy clerks perform their management of cases for 31 judges.

The divisions in my court in which the deputy court clerks work include Civil, Criminal, and Traffic; Probate; Juvenile; Front Office; Small Claims; Domestic and License; Cost Administration; Accounting; Microfilm; and Records and Archives. Deputy court clerks may work in any of these divisions and have various responsibilities depending on which division they are in, although basic responsibilities remain the same. Generally, the larger the city or county, the more divisions an office is likely to have.

One of the most rewarding services that I have provided was in the Small Claims division when I helped an elderly lady initiate her small claims action due to her purchase of a broken refrigerator. The refrigerator did not work after a week and all her food spoiled. The seller would not refund her money. The claimant could not afford a new refrigerator and replace her food, too. I helped her through the small claims and enforcement procedures so that she was able to garnish the seller's bank account and receive her money within the month. She was elated.

Deputy court clerks should remain knowledgeable of new technology on administrative computer use as applied to their positions. They should be intellectually curious with a desire to learn. Because they deal with the public, they should be "people persons" with compassion. Deputy court clerks who wish to improve their abilities, possess excellent organizational skills, and to treat everyone with mutual respect should do well.

A college degree is not required for this profession, but college may enhance a deputy court clerk's ability to receive promotions. Courses of particular use include Computers, Criminal Justice, and other legal related courses such as Civil Procedure, Business, English, and Philosophy. Deputy court clerks may also benefit from membership in local court clerk associations or even national associations, although national associations tend to deal with broader aspects of court management that are not necessarily needed by deputy court clerks.

Overall, I enjoy the diversity of my profession. It is never boring and I experience new and different problems every day.

GETTING IN AND MOVING UP

Deputy court clerk positions are available in city and county courthouses and with the federal government. Every city and county, and the United States government has its own guidelines and procedures for handling employment applications. Many have job hotlines that state positions available for which they seek candidates. By informing the Court Clerk's office that you would like to work, you can be directed to the proper employment office that will provide you with an application. Applications should be typewritten according to the format requested. Generally, you will need to state the position for which you are applying, along with related job codes. Applications should be prepared in a way that will show you possess the right stuff described in this chapter. At the interview, be personable and likeable and demonstrate your efficiency and reliability and you will do well.

Once you are hired by a government entity, you will likely receive more consideration for promotional opportunities than candidates who are not currently in the employ of the government. You should pay particular attention to job opening announcements, if you are interested in promotions or other employment opportunities. If you begin your employment with a city, you may want to seek opportunities with the county or the federal government where salaries are higher. For information on federal clerk opportunities visit *http://www.usajobs.opm.gov* or contact your local directory under U.S. Government.

EMPLOYMENT FORECAST

According to Sally Howe-Smith, "As long as there are courts, there will be Court Clerk offices. Some positions are replaced by technology. Other positions become available due to the increase of court filings and the increasing complexity of litigation." The future employment opportunities as a deputy clerk are very good.

EARNINGS

Yearly earnings throughout the United States average $22,360. Entry-level candidates can expect to earn a range of pay associated with the position and their level of experience, along with benefits that are often not present with other legal employers. The larger the government entity and the larger the population where you work, the more you will likely receive in salary. Sally Howe-Smith says that deputy court clerks with more substantial responsibilities than those associated with entry-level responsibilities earn "approximately $2,769 a month and department heads earn substantially more."

PROFESSIONAL CONNECTIONS

National Association for Court Management
c/o National Center for State Courts
Linda Perkins
300 Newport Avenue (zip code 23185)
P.O. Box 8798
Williamsburg, VA 23187-8798
Tel: (757) 259-1841
(757) 253-2000
Fax: (757) 259-1520
E-mail: nacm@ncsc.dni.us
or lperkins@ncsc.dni.us
Web Site: http://www.nacmnet.org

National Center for State Courts (NCSC)
Court Services Division
300 Newport Avenue
Williamsburg, VA 23185
Tel: (757) 253-2000
Fax: (757) 220-0449

A FEW KEY POINTS TO REMEMBER

• Deputy court clerk positions are available in city, county, and federal courthouses, and with the federal government.

• As a deputy court clerk, you will likely receive stable and secure employment with better benefits than those offered by nongovernment employers.

• Deputy court clerks must be able to deal with the general public and possess high wrist-to-finger speed to process mounds of paperwork, along with having the mental stamina to repeat tasks.

• As a general rule, earnings are highest with the federal government, then the state, county, and municipalities, and the larger the population in your area, the higher your salary will likely be.

CHAPTER ELEVEN

Mediator

According to John Kloiber, Jr., mediator: "The two most rewarding areas for me to mediate involve family/custody and employment disputes. Both of these areas generally involve the continuing relationship of the parties. It is a joy to be a part of helping the parties reach a workable resolution or management plan for their conflict. Most important for the parties is to recognize and acknowledge behavior and communication patterns that cause and heighten conflict, then explore ways that they might make positive improvements in order to resolve or live with the conflict."

In the past five years, most states have passed some type of Alternative Dispute Resolution Act that provides for mediation of disputes because of the expense and time required for litigation and a need for more effective dispute resolution procedures. As Voltaire said, "I was ruined twice in my life. Once when I lost a lawsuit and once when I won one." Participation in the procedure is usually voluntary and referrals to mediation may come from any community source. Some participate involuntarily in the procedure by court order.

Litigation may even be continued during mediation. Almost any type of conflict can be mediated; however, common types of mediation involve landlords and tenants, families, neighbors and friends, employers and employees, perpetrators and victims, roommates, and creditor debtor disputes.

THE RIGHT STUFF

Mediators should assimilate and demonstrate the skills necessary to facilitate effective communication between disputing parties, so that they can help others develop a mutually acceptable solution. Effective mediators will have excellent communication and interpersonal skills. This includes the ability to be objective and not prejudge others. Mediators should exhibit empathy, which is the conscious awareness and consideration of the needs of others, and be able to neutrally present this awareness. This demonstrates mediators' sensitivity to others. Mediators should avoid the use of sympathy which would indicate the sharing of feelings of one party, especially in front of both parties.

Strong communication skills in speaking, listening, and clarifying issues are critical elements of effective communication skills in mediation. This equates to verbal and nonverbal acceptance of each party, along with support and encouragement to the disputants. Mediators should exhibit a desire to understand the conflict instead of hurrying to resolve the matter. They listen by not talking, asking open-ended questions, concentrating, maintaining eye contact, clarifying statements, and not jumping to conclusions.

An ability to deal with people and engender trust and respect through appropriate demeanor assists with effective communication skills. Mediators should remember that communication does not only consist of what a person says, but it also consists of what a disputant does *not* say and his or her body language—what mediators say and communicate through their body language is also important.

Mediators should be able to manage conflict and not shy away from it. In order to facilitate dispute resolution, mediators should be inventive problem solvers, persuasive, and employ distraction techniques when participants become emotional or stray too far from the dispute. Part of a mediator's appeal is the belief that people can solve their own problems. Mediators must supply structure and limits to the process, even with unruly disputants, and know when to terminate a mediation if the disputants refuse to comply.

A broad-based knowledge on substantive issues will help a mediator to address concerns of mediation participants. They should be knowledgable enough to provide disputants information and alternative solutions and feedback about the interaction. The acquisition of negotiation and conflict resolution techniques are required. Mediators should constantly strive to improve their skills and increase their credentials.

No degree is required to become a mediator, but education or training in dispute resolution is desirable. Life experience is helpful along with experience in social work, management, communication, or other conflict resolution professions. The higher the education level and training of mediators, the more knowledgeable they will be. At present, there is no recognizable career path for mediators.

WHAT MEDIATORS DO

According to the Oklahoma Supreme Court *Mediation and Training Resource Manual*, "Mediators use negotiation strategies and interpersonal techniques to assist parties in fashioning agreements and solutions to their problems in a way that each person finds acceptable."

- Mediators assist disputing parties to resolve their conflicts based on their own agreements, instead of by order of a judge or jury verdict. All parties in a dispute participate to reach a decision. Mediators merely facilitate their communications to reach this decision.

- Mediators hear all concerns of parties to a particular dispute and develop creative suggestions to solving disputes, when money is not enough. This is done through a confidential process. Mediation discussions are privileged from disclosure unless a suit is initiated against a mediator or a court order requires otherwise. Of course, if the information could have been acquired in another way, it will not be subject to the privilege.

- Mediators control the flow of information and encourage effective communication by discouraging blaming and defensive or other unproductive behavior, and paraphrasing statements of parties to ensure that they hear each other and respond appropriately.

Mediation is a structured process. There are five typical stages in a mediation that may flow chronologically or overlap each other to some extent.

STAGE I

Mediation Stage I contains the mediator's soliloquy of introductory comments and explanations of the process, along with ground rules. First, mediators will welcome the participants and congratulate them and encourage them about their decision to engage in the process. They will describe the disputants' purpose and their own role. The parties will be told about confidentiality and reminded that their participation is voluntary and they can terminate the mediation at any time. The parties are also reminded that litigation generally results in a win/lose resolution by a stranger and compromise involves a lose/lose situation. However, in mediation, the parties may fashion a resolution that is a win/win situation for all parties involved. The five-stage process described here is explained to the parties.

Mediators will ask if they can call the parties by their first names. The parties must be treated equitably during this phase and all mediation phases. In the spirit of equitable treatment, if one disputant prefers to be addressed by a surname, then all disputants must be addressed by surnames. When ground rules are discussed, mediators should ask each party individually if they agree to each ground rule. These rules include not speaking unless it is one's turn, and addressing all comments to the mediator instead of the other party, as well as others.

STAGE II

In Stage II problem determination occurs when each party presents his or her side of the dispute. Mediators may ask clarification questions and paraphrase the statements made. During this stage, the parties commonly forget the ground rules and interrupt. Mediators must then establish the limits and structure for the discussion by reminding both parties of the ground rules, instead of just the infringing party. It is important that mediators not single out one party for reprimand. Parties must be encouraged and supported when they listen and be reminded that they will receive equal treatment and time to present the facts. Both parties should be congratulated for their progress and participation throughout this process.

Mediators should then state areas of similarity between the disputants and set priorities for the resolution of the conflict along with stating the intention to resolve the matter. Mediators may ask clarifying questions as long as they are not asked in a confrontational manner.

STAGE III

During Stage III, the parties generate and evaluate alternative resolutions for each other. Without a mediator's help the process would usually stop at this point. After asking each party what they want to resolve the conflict, mediators state similarities in the proposals. Sometimes, at this stage, mediators will need to separate the parties in order to help them ascertain the strengths and weaknesses of their proposals in what is known as "reality testing."

STAGE IV

If a resolution is agreed upon, mediators enter Stage IV of the mediation process that requires them to acquire specifics of the agreement. Mediators should establish what, who, when, where, and how. This generally means that mediators should determine what each party will do, when they will do it, in what manner, and where, in a reciprocal manner. For example, if one party agrees to pay the other $1,000 and the other party agrees to accept the money and dismiss the suit, then a mediator should discuss the form of payment and when payments will be made, where they will be sent and when, and how the other party will dismiss the litigation.

STAGE V

During Stage V, the mediator drafts a simple agreement that all parties sign. This agreement contains reciprocal obligations upon each party with the specifics for performance. The agreement should be simple and understandable. It should also be drafted in the positive in that each party is stated "to agree to" some act. It should state that all matters related to the dispute are resolved and contain any necessary future provisions.

Overall, mediators listen, ask questions, and probe for solutions during this process. They aid parties in structuring agreements. The parties are responsible for their agreement and a mediator may not force parties to settle or make decisions for the parties. It is critical that mediators make disputants aware of this to ensure that they will bear the responsibility for the agreements, and increases the likelihood that the disputants will comply with their agreements after they leave the mediation.

Mediators may terminate the session at any time, if a disputant is unwilling or unable to make an effort to meaningfully participate. If a party is irrational, intoxicated, or exhibits impaired judgment, mediation should be terminated. If domestic abuse or an excessive imbalance of power is present, mediators may need to terminate a session. Mediators do not offer legal advice and must report revelations of abuse and neglect.

WHAT THE JOB IS *REALLY* LIKE

A typical day for a busy mediator involves scheduling mediations and reviewing mediation statements and other documents, identifying and attending career enhancement opportunities through training and curriculum, and volunteering time for organizations in dispute resolution. When a day is booked with one or generally no more than two paid mediations, the mediator spends his or her day in the dispute resolution process previously described.

According to John Kloiber, Jr., mediator, his typical day varies: "When I have a mediation scheduled, I arrive at a designated location and spend two to six hours helping parties resolve their dispute. Usually, I begin Postal EEO (Equal Employment Opportunity) mediations at 7:00 A.M. Around 1:30 P.M., I begin a court-ordered mediation and in the evening I will conduct a volunteer custody mediation. On other days, I wait for the phone to ring. If the phone doesn't ring, there is very little work to do. Record keeping is very minimal in the mediation profession. There is often premediation preparation. Time is also spent making people aware of my services, giving time to professional organizations, volunteering as a mediator for those unable to pay for services, and attending continuing education seminars."

A Person
Who's Done It

MEET JOHN KLOIBER, JR.

VITAL STATISTICS

John Kloiber, Jr. is a mediator with six years of experience and more than 255 mediations to date. Prior to becoming a mediator, he was a certified purchasing manager. He became interested in mediation when he heard his wife, who is an attorney, speaking about mediation with a friend.

He has many state-based certifications, including specialty certifications in Family and Divorce, Agricultural Commission, and Workers' Compensation certifications, and has been approved as mediator for the Western District Federal Court. He is also a certified redress mediator for Equal Employment Opportunity cases against the United States Postal Service. With 189½ hours of training offered through local universities and state and federal agencies, he now coaches others on how to mediate. Since 1994 he has attended approximately 19 continuing education courses in the field of mediation. He does not have a college degree, but he has taken a substantial number of undergraduate courses and is a candidate for a Master of Arts in Conflict Resolution at Antioch University. Recently, he was selected to sit on a panel of arbitrators who have *the authority to determine the just result of a dispute with the same force and effect of a judicial judgment. Here is his story.*

My career is one of conflict resolution and management. Although a lawsuit is not necessary in order to enter into mediation, many court-ordered mediations and other parties embroiled in litigation do seek mediators. However, all that is necessary in order to mediate is a dispute. The mediations I conduct generally involve debt collections, divorce and custody, discrimination and retaliation matters with the U.S. Postal Service, personal injury, and landlord-tenant and property disputes. I have also handled workers' compensation, medical malpractice, community, parent/teen, employment, assault and battery, guardianship, and attorney fee dispute mediations.

I'm not sure exactly when I decided to become a mediator; it was a process. I heard about mediation from my wife, and was interested enough to take some training, and then get some experience through state-based volunteer organizations. As I mediated and saw the win/win solutions that were possible, I knew I wanted to continue in this field. As opposed to litigation or other power-driven methods of conflict resolution where a solution is imposed on the parties, mediation offers the parties the opportunity to meet everyone's interests. In litigation, most frequently one of the parties is unhappy with the result and often, no one is completely satisfied.

Prior experiences have helped me in the field of mediation. My 11-year grocery management career helped sharpen my preexisting love of people. I enjoyed learning my customers' names and interesting facts about them. I became a true "people person." Many years spent in industrial purchasing management exposed me to issues involved in business-to-business transactions. Both jobs helped me to have hands-on experience with employer/employee problems and their solutions.

Finally, I divorced and fought a custody battle in the court system. My former wife and I were both unhappy with the court order after spending huge amounts of time and money. We fashioned a post-divorce agreement between ourselves that was workable and that we abided by for 15 years without court involvement. I believe that this personal experience cemented my belief that individuals are often better off working out their own solutions and conflict management programs.

Becoming a mediator is very tough; one has to be dedicated and persistent. Some people will not give respect to a mediator without a college degree, but, most people merely want to be sure that he or she has the mediation training and experience to be able to help them with their dispute. After they are convinced of this, they will not spend much time thinking about the mediator, but will be totally engaged in their conflict. My interest, training, dedication, and commitment to the profession caused me to seek more education. Without an undergraduate degree, I was accepted into the Master of Arts program in Conflict Resolution at Antioch University and will complete it within six to nine months. Thus, not only is it possible to practice mediation without a degree, it may cause you to pursue one to gain greater knowledge.

Mediators have to be impartial. They should expect to have personal biases surface during mediations, but the challenge is to keep these to themselves, so that they do not influence the parties. Mediators should be willing and able to let the parties fashion an agreement that they believe will work for them. If the parties need legal advice during mediation, they should have their attorneys present in person or by telephone. Mediators should not give legal advice, especially if they are not attorneys. They should like people, and not be afraid of conflict. Mediators who themselves do not like conflict, will often try to smooth things over too quickly before the parties have achieved their best solution or conflict management plan.

I believe the future of mediation is bright. More and more people, and the courts, are becoming aware of the positive benefits of mediation. This is especially true when the parties' relationship will continue by chance or choice, regardless of the dispute outcome. In such situations, mediation is by far the better way to address disputes.

There are mediation opportunities in various federal government agencies. I have signed a two-year agreement to provide mediation services for the United States Postal Service. The Equal Employment Opportunity Commission also employs contract mediators. Most states have different organizations or agencies that provide for mediators and their services; some pay the mediators for their services, but others do not. For example, the

Oklahoma Supreme Court has an Early Settlement Program. Through this program, any approved applicant interested in mediation can acquire training and certification to perform mediations on a volunteer basis. This is the route I took to begin training and gain experience. However, many volunteer organizations do not provide learning or training on how to mediate professionally, because they are vested in keeping mediation as volunteer work. There may be a similar organization in your area that can teach you the ropes of how to mediate.

I have chosen to hang out my own shingle. I rely on referrals, my contract with the Postal Service, repeat clients, and my reputation to bring the work to me.

There are many training opportunities nationally. Many, such as CDR Associates in Boulder, Colorado, are excellent. There are some training providers in each state. Some of these providers are associated with colleges and universities. There are private providers as well. It is very important to be sure that training provides opportunities for mediation observations and experience. Under the two main acts covering mediation in Oklahoma—the District Court Mediation Act and the Alternative Dispute Resolution Act—training, observations, and experience are required for certification. You should investigate any state acts applicable to your practice as a mediator in your local area.

GETTING IN AND MOVING UP

Mediators do not need formal training but may be required to receive certifications or accreditations in the districts in which they work. Many courts are now requiring parties to try mediation before trial. With the proper court approval, if required, you can become a mediator. Many mediators have backgrounds in law, psychology, social work, counseling, religion, or finance. Of all areas of mediation specialties, family mediators must acquire the highest level of training in order to handle emotional and sometimes volatile disputes between family members. Public mediators are carefully screened, but any private mediator can hang out a shingle and profess to be a mediator. Prospective mediators should obtain basic foundational training, observe sessions, then be observed and conduct co-mediations before attempting to mediate alone.

President Joseph Paulk of Dispute Resolution Consultants, Inc worked as an attorney for 19 years until he opted for a professional career exclusively in mediation in 1999. He has received training from premier programs through-out the United States at Harvard University, Pepperdine University, and the American Law Institute. He conducts training seminars and speeches on mediation, negotiation, and conflict resolution throughout the country and as an adjunct professor at the University of Arkansas and University of Tulsa. He has written a variety of articles on mediation. Mr. Paulk advises those who want to get into this profession without a college degree to "become involved with a community-based mediation program and investigate mediation oppor-tunities at your local Better Business Bureau."

He says, "You should begin wherever anyone will give you a chance, even if you are not paid for your services. Regardless of whether or not you have a degree starting out, you will be upside down financially for training: You will have to give away your services for free in the beginning. You can obtain initial training and experience through a plethora of groups and organizations for profit and not for profit that train people on advance mediation services."

He advises that the most important part of being an effective mediator is to first, have listening skills, then second, have patience. Finally, he recom-mends that mediators "be directional without being judgmental. You want to help parties move forward and compromise by recognizing not just legal posi-tions, but also personal and financial ones."

He also says, "It is very difficult for lawyers to hire non-lawyers. They will usually require postgraduate education, so if you want to cater to this group, you have to take strengths and life experiences and play them up with market-ing. Lack of education will become obvious, so you must differentiate your-self. Experience in such specific niche business as computers, trucking, or oil can set you apart. Insurance companies and legal professions generate the most mediation opportunities, but other opportunities exist as well."

While obtaining mediation training, you will be exposed to a variety of dif-ferent models. Joseph Paulk says, "There are as many mediation models as there are styles. Mediation is in the eye of the beholder. I do not use a model because the most important aspect of a mediator is to be flexible. You must be able to get a sense of what is going on instead of being rigidly set to a specific model. Whether or not a mediator should apply pressure or back off is a matter of instinct and reading body language for me. The evaluative model of mediation may require a mediator to come down hard on a disputant; mediators should have the ability to go to that, if necessary."

He advises those in mediation "to investigate whether the local bar association has a section on Alternative Dispute Resolution that they can join. Often, you will not have to be a lawyer to join. Also, by becoming a member in the Society of Professionals in Dispute Resolution (SPIDR), you will have instant credibility."

Mediators must be able to handle difficult situations during mediations in order to gain a reputation and more clients. In times of trouble, a good mediator will echo statements or ask questions, confirm agreements with specifics, write agreements using the words of the parties, never give up a mediation without several attempts, and recognize when resolution is not achievable. A good mediator will never ask disputants what they think. Mediators will handle interruptions by ignoring them, placing their hand up as if to say "Stop," ask parties to help them listen, remind parties that they are there to help and they agreed not to interrupt in the ground rules. Good mediators will also know when breaking up the parties into individual caucuses is more efficient. Many times this is the case if the parties will not have a continuing relationship after the resolution, if a large amount of money is at stake, if the mediation is court ordered and not a small claims matter, if there are hidden agendas, or if the dispute is emotionally charged.

EMPLOYMENT FORECAST

Because this field is so new and courts are beginning to order mediation more often, this profession is expected to grow dramatically in the next ten years. You can find out more information about future employment opportunities in mediation at these web sites.

Academy of Family Mediators	*http://www.mediators.org/*
The Association of Attorney-Mediators Online	*http://www.attorney-mediators.org/*
The Family Mediators Association	*http://www.familymediators.co.uk/*
Tennessee Mediators Network	*http://www.tnmediators.com/*
American College of Civil Trial Mediators	*http://www.acctm.org/*
Directory of Professional Mediators	*http://www.mediators.net/DirMed.htm*
Online Mediators Home	*http://www.onlinemediators.com/*
Information Mediators AS	*http://www.imas.no/*
PA Council of Mediators	*http://www.libertynet.org/pcounmed/*
Texas Association of Mediators	*http://www.txmediator.org/*
NJ Association of Professional Mediators (NJAPM)	*http://www.njapm.org/*
Oklahoma Academy of Mediators and Arbitrators	*http://www.oama.org/*
Colorado Mediation	*http://www.coloradomediation.org/*
Lex Mundi College of Mediators—Code of Ethics for Mediators	*http://www.lexmundi.org/med-ethics.html*
Mediation Materials and Comprehensive Contents for Mediators	*http://adrr.com/toc.htm*
Model Standards of Conduct for Mediators	*http://www.adr.org/rules/ethics/standard.html*
Illinois Mediation, Mediators, and ADR Resources	*http://www.mediationnow.com/IL/default.htm*
Divorce Source: Divorce Professionals: About Divorce Mediators and Therapists/	*http://www.divorcesource.com/info/professionals/mediators.shtml*
Dispute Resolution Standards	*http://www.mediate.com/ethics*
International Academy of Mediators	*http://www.iamed.org/about_the_academy.htm*

EARNINGS

Mediator fees vary by location, but hourly rates ranging from $25 to $250 an hour are common. John Kloiber suggests that, after two years of part-time mediation work, one can expect earnings in excess of $20,000 a year; in five to six years, the income can increase to $30,000 a year. Others say that mediators with a high level of experience and an established client base (and who do not have a college degree) can expect to earn $40,000 to $50,000 a year. If a mediator's experience and geographic location allow higher hourly rates, they can expect incomes in excess of $200,000 a year.

PROFESSIONAL CONNECTIONS

The American Academy of Family Mediators (AFM)
5 Militia Drive
Lexington, MA 02421
Tel: (800) 292-4AFM
(781) 674-2663
Fax: (781) 674-2690
E-mail: *afmoffice@mediators.org*
Web Site: *http://www.mediators.org*

The Council of Better Business Bureaus (CBBB)
4200 Wilson Blvd., Suite 800
Arlington, VA 22203-1838
Tel: (800) 334-2406, ext 383
(703) 276-0100
Fax: (703) 525-8277
E-mail: *bbb@bbb.org*
Web Site: *http://www.bbb.org*

National ADR Resource Center (Information Service)
Ms. Sue K. Dosal
State Court Administrator
Supreme Court of Minnesota
135 Minnesota Judicial Center

25 Constitution Avenue
St. Paul, MN 55155
Tel: (612) 296-2474

National Association For Community Mediation (NAFCM)
1527 New Hampshire Avenue, NW
Washington, DC 20036-1206
Tel: (202) 667-9700
Fax: (202) 667-8629
E-mail: *nafcm@nafcm.org*
Web Site: *http://www.nafcm.org*

Society of Professionals in Dispute Resolution (SPIDR)
1527 New Hampshire Avenue, NW, Third Floor
Washington, D.C. 20036
Tel: (202) 667-9700
Fax: (202) 265-1968
E-mail: *spidr@spidr.org*
Web Site: *http://www.spidr.org*

A FEW KEY POINTS TO REMEMBER

• Mediators are active listeners who are soft on people and hard on problems, acquire ideas, facts, and feelings with reciprocal empathy, and encourage and support participants to solve their own problems.

• Mediators do not offer legal advice.

• Mediators employ conflict resolution and negotiation techniques along with their mediation training.

• The future employment opportunities are high for this new profession.

CHAPTER TWELVE

Legal Support Providers

There are many other law-related careers besides those already discussed in this book. These include careers as bailiffs, insurance claims clerks and adjusters, bail bondsmen, process servers, law librarians, receptionists, runners, file clerks, translators and interpreters, and title researchers, abstractors, and examiners. Most of these professions are quite similar to other professions discussed in this book and require similar job skills. Refer to related sections for more information.

BAILIFFS

"All rise! Court is now in session!" Bailiffs announce that the court is in session immediately preceding the judge's entry into the courtroom. Bailiffs were formerly known as court criers and are being replaced in the federal courts by U.S. Marshals; however, state courts still commonly employ them. A bailiff acts as the right hand of a judge and is present at all courtroom proceedings to maintain order by ensuring that everyone in the courtroom acts appropriately and by ejecting those who do not. Bailiffs assist witnesses with seating and in the dissemination of exhibits. They also ensure the sequestration of witnesses and assist with other court docketing and scheduling orders.

Many bailiffs believe the best part of their jobs is learning firsthand how a judge routinely operates and rules, and witnessing different attorneys' litigation styles. Bailiffs should generally give a presence and formality to court proceedings, as they are there to maintain order. They are particularly used in criminal litigation matters.

Overall, the job prospects for the position of bailiff are not good, as the trend is to replace bailiffs with law enforcement personnel. Check in your local area to determine the requirements for employment.

INSURANCE CLAIMS CLERKS AND ADJUSTERS

Each state has certain licensing requirements for insurance adjusters. If you are interested in this profession, contact your State Insurance Commissioner for more information. Generally, an insurance adjuster must be at least 18 years old and pass a written examination along with the filing of a public adjusters' bond. Conditions of the bond include that you will faithfully comply with state law and shall not fraudulently withhold any money owed to an insured, or your license may be revoked.

Insurance claims clerks and adjusters handle claims services for losses or damages arising out of insurance, surety, or indemnity policies on property, people, or businesses. Insurance adjusters perform work similar to that of a private investigator, legal secretary, and legal assistant combined. They are often the equivalent of legal assistants, but deal more with prelitigation. In other words, an insurance adjuster is to an insurance defense attorney much as a legal assistant is to a personal injury attorney. Once litigation begins, they serve as the liaison between counsel and the company. Insurance claims clerks and adjusters learn how to investigate claims as a private investigator might, to a more limited degree.

Insurance claims clerks and adjusters provide litigation assessments with claim evaluations, and negotiate settlements. They or their assistants request and assemble medical records regarding personal injury claims or life insurance claims. They even investigate arson on homeowner policies and negligent performance of contractual or professional duties. They must review insurance policies and confirm that policy provisions provide coverage. Also, they evaluate whether the claims for damages submitted are appropriate, and calculate benefits. Insurance adjusters and their assistants must learn about insurance law and administration and how to handle claims.

The average annual job opening due to growth and total replacement need from 1998 to 2000 for insurance adjusters, examiners, and investigators is 16,000 jobs a year. In 1998 there were a total of 180,000 jobs; in 2008 it is estimated there will be 217,000 jobs. The unemployment rate for insurance adjusters will be very low but many insurance adjusters must have bachelor's degrees or experience that can be acquired through the acquisition of an entry-level position and working their way up. The overall employment forecast for insurance adjusters and their assistants is very good.

BAIL BONDSMEN

Bail bondsmen post bail with a court to ensure a particular defendant's appearance. Under the bond requirements, a defendant is obligated to appear at every court hearing. If a defendant does not appear, the entire amount of the bond is owed by the bail bondsman or agent. Defendants generally pay 10 percent of the bail bond for a bondsman's guarantee of their appearance. Bail bondsmen may face bankruptcy if a bond is large enough and they cannot locate a defendant. When defendants do not appear at court, bail bondsmen must search for them or hire a bounty hunter to locate them if the bond is high enough.

A successful bail bondsman should be able to talk to people, interact with them, and determine whether a defendant is telling the truth. If a defendant gives false information, there is a possibility they will not appear in court, and, of course, the bail bondsman should not process the loan.

Most states require state licensure and annual training in order to work as a bail bondsman. In order to begin a career as a bail bondsman, either as an agent of an organization or self-employed, you should first check with your local authorities regarding proper licensure.

Joe Valencia, bail agent, has been a bail bondsman for three years. He works for Josh Herman, "the bail bondsman of choice for jailed rap stars." He is responsible for answering the phones, writing bonds, processing paperwork, and talking to clients. "My agency deals with many celebrities and has affiliations with several record companies to help their musicians in times of trouble. Many bail bondsmen advertise to the general public, but we work with a more upscale clientele." Most bail bondsmen cater to the general public and advertise to potential clients through billboard advertising and other media likely to reach the more troubled people in society.

PROCESS SERVERS

Process servers perform work similar to that of private investigators, except that their work is limited to locating people and serving papers on them. This can be a time-consuming process if a process server must wait for someone or devise creative methods to get someone to answer their door. Process servers must also have access to databases to determine the whereabouts of individuals to be served.

After serving the papers, they file proof of service with the courts. Every state and U.S District Court has different requirements to effectuate service, and process servers should be familiar with all those applicable laws. Private process servers learn the legal requirements for serving papers. The private investigator's activities and job requirements are similar to that of a process server or bail bondsman and state licensure is required.

LAW LIBRARIANS

General librarians should know how to find information. Legal research is the most difficult and complicated of all the types of research available. Law librarians learn every facet of this ever so critical facet of legal practice—legal research. Legal research is an invaluable tool for law office professionals, and especially legal assistants. If you want to learn all about where to find statutes and cases, how to use digests and key cite information, how to find regulations and legislative court records, and how to find treatises or articles on particular topics, a law librarian can help. Law librarians routinely help people find what they are looking for in card catalogs and other indexes. They shelve and catalog books or other materials, check out books, assist with sometimes bungled copy efforts, and handle other administrative matters.

As a librarian, and especially a law librarian, you can master the art of research and even the investigation of people and entities. Because research and investigation constitute much of the work required in legal professions, most employers would welcome the legal research expertise of a law librarian. For more information about librarians visit these web sites.

American Association of Libraries	http://www.aallnet.org/index.asp
American Library Association	http://www.ala.org/education
Association of Research Libraries	http://db.arl.org/careers
Librarians Job Search Source	http://www.lisjobs.com

Librarians who work for the federal government average $56,370 a year, in city government they average $39,456 a year, and in county government, they average $40,694 a year. There are also many employment opportunities with law schools, as well as opportunities for freelance law librarians to maintain small to medium-sized law firm libraries. Many of the larger law firms have a full-time law librarian on salary to maintain their books, periodicals, and other materials.

RECEPTIONISTS

A law office receptionist is the one person with whom all office employees and clients should interact. Receptionists are privy to most of a firm's activities and gain a general overall knowledge of issues of legal practice and administration. With experience, many tasks commonly delegated to legal secretaries, legal assistants, legal marketers, and law office administrators may be delegated to a receptionist in preparation for a promotion.

As a receptionist, you would have to learn how to deal with difficult attorneys and clients. You should remain composed and friendly at all times, with a pleasant voice for callers. By taking messages and speaking with callers, you would learn legal terminology and effective client relations. You may also be assigned other typically secretarial tasks such as typing, entering billing for attorneys, or ordering supplies.

RUNNERS

As a runner for a firm you would file pleadings and ensure that motions and orders are delivered to judges and picked up once they are signed. You would also have to run a variety of other errands necessary for the law office, much like a courier. Through this experience, you would meet many legal professionals and learn basic court procedures, including the number of copies needed and what should accompany pleadings in order for them to be filed. Many runners also double as file clerks, or a file clerk may be a separate position with a law firm, depending upon the size of the firm. Runners learn the written format of documents in the legal arena and have exposure to legal terminology and the operation of a law office. Many law students seek first-time legal jobs as runners because it allows them the opportunity to learn the ropes of procedure and courthouse operations. Other aspiring legal professionals also may welcome a runner's position with the same expectations.

FILE CLERKS

File clerks are responsible for maintaining and organizing the files of a law office or other organization and they learn about the types of documents that should be maintained in a legal file. Filing systems may be organized by client name or an assigned number. These are filed in order and may be color coded according to the attorney or practice group to whom each case is assigned or by type of case. Client information cards may need to be completed for insertion into the client files, electronic case management software, or for other databases. File clerks may type pleading indexes and three-holepunch documents, and add tabs to each corresponding number on an index. They separate final pleadings from mere drafts, correspondence, and evidence, and ensure that the pleading files match the court files, complete with file stamps on all pleadings. File clerks also close files in order to prepare them for storage after a case has been completed for a year or more. They must number storage boxes, list closed files on an index, and transport them to storage.

File clerks must ensure that all documents are readily available and locatable when they are needed by others. They also organize receipts and statements generated by a firm or other organization. File clerks must be organized and efficient and able to immediately procure a specific document for others when requested. File maintenance and organization is one of the best ways to begin learning about how a law firm operates.

TRANSLATORS AND INTERPRETERS

If you are fluent in a foreign language, you may want to investigate becoming a translator and interpreter in the legal field. Court translators restate *verbatim* precisely what is said in a court proceeding. It is imperative that a translator or interpreter restate *exactly* what is said and be knowledgeable about the translation of legal terminology. Translators are also retained to transcribe pleadings, especially discovery requests, from English to a client's native tongue.

Many self-employment opportunities exist for those translators and interpreters who are interested in translating legal documents.

TITLE SEARCHERS, ABSTRACTORS, AND EXAMINERS

Title research involves investigation of public databases for the compilation of a complete list of all instruments pertaining to title of a particular piece of property. Documents that may be compiled include liens, mortgages, contracts, bills of sale, judgments, and deeds. In any form of title opinion work, professionals must carefully compare sometimes lengthy and complicated property descriptions to ensure that they are absolutely identical in all respects to all documents compiled and any and all new documents created. If this has not been correctly done in the past, the chain of title the examiner investigates may be invalid or future transfer of title may be invalidated. Title examiners and abstractors review the compiled documents, assemble them, and draft detailed lists of all documents compiled and restrictions on the use of the property that may be contained within those instruments.

If you work for a title and abstract company, you may draft abstracts and examine claims of title. Title examiners or abstractors may recommend that actions are needed to clear the title. A title researcher examines and abstracts, and must have knowledge of real estate procedures in order to draft a closing statement and issue a final policy of title insurance. The average yearly earnings for these professionals is $25,792. They generally perform many of the tasks a legal assistant would, except that such tasks and any required legal research are limited to property and real estate laws.

THE BENEFITS OF EXPERIENCE IN THE LEGAL PROFESSION

The law touches every aspect of our lives and professions. There are so many positions available that will deal to some extent with the law that it is impossible to name them all.

- If you work as a purchasing assistant, you will negotiate and draft contracts.

- If you work in human resources you will deal with employment discrimination and other labor law issues.

- Accountants deal with tax laws daily and audits by the IRS. Employment with government entities will likely require you to know some aspects of law that regulates that particular entity.

Overall, many job experiences you may have had could relate well to a transition into a legal career. If you have a legal career and then decide to transition into a nonlaw-related career, your experience will likely be of use in most professional positions. A careful look at job responsibilities will generally reveal that your prior experience will somehow match with any new professional position you may seek. If you do not know what type of career to try, a legal profession will likely give you a foundation of expertise and knowledge that will make you a viable candidate for the job of your dreams, regardless of whether that future employment is law-related or not.

CHAPTER THIRTEEN

Find the Job That Is Right for You

A spiring legal professionals should evaluate their career options. Each profession will likely require an initial time investment of low pay and a willingness to increase qualifications through education, training, and certifications. If you are an aspiring legal professional, you should consider whether your personal traits, habits, and characteristics lend themselves to a successful career. By the creation of a list of personal traits in order of competency and career preferences carefully prioritized, you may compare your abilities with those discussed in this text and required in the professions discussed here.

EVALUATE CAREER OPTIONS

Finding legal employment could be a task. Initially, you should decide what type of profession you would eventually like to have, then you should assess the type of employment for which you qualify now. If this is not the profession you ultimately want, you should determine what type of position will best prepare you for eventual employment in your field of choice. Here are some other considerations that you should investigate.

1. **Do you want a law firm or organization as an employer?**
   Approximately 78 percent of all attorneys enter private practice. Thus, many more traditional career opportunities are in private firm practice or devoted to services for private practice law firms. Potential employers of legal professionals, excluding private practice firms, include the following.

   - Governments, including courthouses, judges, district attorneys' offices, and public defender offices

   - Law schools, paralegal schools, and legal secretarial schools

   - Corporations

   - Military

   - Alternative Dispute Resolution organizations

   - Insurance groups

   - Legislatures and executive offices

   - Libraries

   - Title and abstract companies

   - Mortgage companies and other lending organizations

   - Bill collection agencies

- Marketing and advertising

- Self-employment opportunities

2. **Is the size of the firm or organization important?** If it is, you should search according to your preference. Smaller firms or organizations tend to be more individualized than larger ones but offer lower pay and fewer benefits. However, the larger the firm, the more prestigious it tends to be, with higher pay and better benefits. A large firm could operationally be equivalent to a small one if you work with only a select group of attorneys and staff. By looking at the size of firms entered by attorneys, legal professionals can gauge where the most employment opportunities are. Since approximately 68 percent of all new attorneys enter firms that have fewer than 20 attorneys, there are likely more employment opportunities at smaller firms. However, if you live in a major metropolitan area that has several conglomerate law firms, this may not hold true. These statistics show that the odds of gaining employment are higher with smaller firms.

3. **Is there is a particular area of law in which you would like to work?** Areas of law commonly include corporate and business law, employment law, family law, personal injury and medical malpractice, estate planning and probate, bankruptcy, administrative law, elder law, juvenile justice, criminal law, insurance law, and constitutional law, to name a few. You should find a job that will allow you to work in some capacity in the area of law in which you would like exposure.

4. **Do you have a preference for litigation- or nonlitigation-type of work?** Although most legal work is paper-intensive, litigation work tends to have more time pressure due to filing deadlines than nonlitigation work. Litigation work also involves more contact with clients who are frequently frantic and emotional. Those who do not want to deal with clients as often, could prefer nonlitigation work in

drafting wills and trusts, corporate minutes, or title opinions and abstracts. However, it is easier to change jobs from a litigation support position to a nonlitigation position, and generally, you will likely acquire more experiences related to other professions in a litigation support role.

If you are unable to pursue the career of your choice, you should consider an alternate; for example, starting off as a filing clerk instead of a legal secretary may not be such a bad idea, especially if you are working with a law firm or an insurance company. This experience will educate you about what legal professions are really like and whether it is an option that you truly want. You will become familiar with pleadings and correspondence, and attendant legal terminology and it will help you get your foot in the door. Eventually, your responsibilities will include those of other positions and you will receive a promotion or be more qualified for the next job hunt.

MARKET YOURSELF

Prospective legal job candidates should investigate all posted career opportunities in classified ads, on the Internet, at local schools, and in the state and/or county bar journals. A state's bar journal is often the best source of job listings and finding out about the local legal community. Applicants should subscribe to their state bar journal to keep tabs on employment opportunities as well as legal news. Other methods to gain insightful job leads include

- career services at your alma mater and other schools.

- Internet job hunting.

- networking.

- headhunters.

- directories of corporate information.

- newspapers, local and national.

- temporary agencies and other employment agencies.

- Martindale-Hubbell Lawyer Locator.

- Westlaw and Lexis.

The current trend in employment is applicant selection through the Internet and computerized applicant tracking systems. Most law firms do not yet utilize these resources but the trend is that in the future they will. Therefore, unless you live in a large metropolitan area, you should probably use bar journals, newspaper, and temporary agencies to locate potential employers. However, other organizations and companies have legal departments that do utilize this technology. The larger and more technologically advanced an organization is, the more likely it will use cyberspace to locate potential employees.

In cyberspace, you can locate many available positions with different organizations in legal fields. Many potential employers have web sites that allow applicants to post their résumés directly on their site. Other general career-related web sites allow applicants to research available positions and post their résumés. Here are some of the general career Internet sites.

America's Job Bank	http://www.ajb.dni.us
The Brass Ring	http://www.BrassRing.com
Bridges Online	http://www.bridgesonline.com
CareerBuilder	http://www.careerbuilder.com
Career Adviser	http://www.careeradviser.com
CareerCity	http://www.careercity.com
Career Mosaic	http://www.careermosaic.com
CareerPath	http://www.careerpath.com
CareerShop.com	http://wwit.careershop.com

Headhunter.net	http://www.headhunter.net
HotJobs.com	http://www.hotjobs.com
InfoWorks	http://www.it123.com
JobOptions	http://www/joboptions.com
JobTrak	http://www.jobtrak.com
Monster.com	http://www.monster.com
MyJobSearch.com	http://www.myjobsearch.com
NationJob Network	http://www.nationjob.com
Net-Temps	http://www.net-temps.com
Virtual Job Fair	http://www.vjf.com/
WorkTree.com	http://www.worktree.com

Here are career Internet sites that are exclusively law related.

Arbitration Services	http://www.adr.com
Career Center (Paralegals)	http://www.paralegals.org/Center/home.html
The Federal Judiciary	http://www.uscourts.com
Judiciary Job Opportunities	http://www.judiciary.state.nj.us/jobs/index.htm
The Law Employment Center	http://class.ljx.com
Law Jobs Career Center	http://www.lawjobs.com
Law Mail Resume Center	http://www.lawmall.com/resumes/resumes.html
Law News Network	http://www.lawnewsnetwork.com
Law Offices (West's Legal Directory)	http://www.lawoffice.com
LegaldotNet	http://db.legal.net/ldn/welcome/query.cfm
Martindale-Hubbell Lawyer Locator	http://www.martindale.com/locator/home.html
National Federation of Paralegals Association	http://www.paralegals.com
U.S. Department of Justice	http://www.usdoj.gov/06employment/index.html
Update Legal	http://www.updatelegal.com/legal.asp
Verbatim Court Reporters	http://www.verbatimreporters.com

Pat Criscito, author of Barron's *Résumés in Cyberspace*, has a list of other Internet sites at *http://www.patcriscito.com*.

By engaging in activities described in prior chapters about particular fields, you will be well on your way to marketing yourself for positions.

EVALUATE OFFERS

Attorneys are devising more and more unusual pay structures and arrangements. If you are hired as an independent contractor, you will be responsible for taxes that would have been paid by your employer, in addition to the taxes you would usually pay. Further, as an independent consultant, you will likely receive no benefits including sick pay or vacation time. Here are some factors you should review when considering an offer of employment as an independent contractor.

- Salary

- Association fees

- Examination fees

- Membership fees

- Continuing education fees and expenses

- Medical

- 401(K) Plan

- Paid vacation and sick leave

- Tuition reimbursement

- Health club fees

- Other educational fees

- Other benefits

If you have little or no experience, you should be primarily concerned with gaining entry into your chosen profession and whether a potential employer will provide you with an appropriate opportunity for training and guidance, instead of salary or benefits. The income and benefits will come with increased experience, training, and education.

A FEW KEY POINTS TO REMEMBER

- Prioritize your career interests and capabilities and determine which career is right for you.
- The best ways to learn about available positions is through state bar journals, the newspaper, and legal temporary agencies.
- Do not forget to investigate cyber opportunities to market yourself and seek out potential employers.
- When evaluating offers, do not underestimate the value of experience in entering a new profession. Experience must be acquired before you realize the benefits of higher pay and other peaks such as health and life insurance, vacation and paid holidays, and various allowances.

CHAPTER FOURTEEN

Get the Job You Want

C over letters and résumés are sales techniques designed to promote applicants to employers through their knowledge of the industry, company, or organization, and job responsibilities. Interviews are the candidates' in-person sales opportunity. What are candidates' selling? Themselves. When you seek employment, you must sell yourself to the employer. As an entry-level candidate, you may do this by concentrating on the position available and your qualifications for it, as a salesman focuses on a product being sold. The more experience, training, and education you have, the more you will be expected to know about the industry and the firm or organization. The better your sales job during the résumé and interview process, the more the tables will turn and the employer will try to sell *you* on the position. Only after you have sold yourself to an employer will salary and benefits be discussed.

CREATE A POWERFUL FIRST IMPRESSION: RESUMES AND COVER LETTERS

Your cover letter and résumé tell a story about you. You will be evaluated constantly from the time your résumé is reviewed and throughout your tenure with a firm or organization. Upon preliminary review of candidates for a position, most employers will read cover letters, then review the employer names and former job titles contained in the résumés. If this seems acceptable, they will then look to see how long the candidate was employed at each position. Then, if this preliminary review shows a viable candidate, they will study the objective statement. When a candidate's cover letter and résumé pass these inspection stages, an employer will read candidate résumés in more detail.

When potential employers review stacks of résumés, they form an initial opinion about each candidate based upon their résumé and cover letter. They base their opinion, not only on the substantive content of candidates' résumés, but also on formatting, grammar, punctuation, and writing style. Obviously, if the formatting is unattractive and you use improper grammar and punctuation, it is unlikely you will get an interview. For example, if you use improper verb tense in a sentence such as, "I been a secretary for 3 years," a prospective employer will likely think you are uneducated and unprofessional. This may lead to a more detailed belief that you would produce sloppy work, not pay attention to details, and look for ineffective shortcuts. Not only does the improper verb tense in the sentence support this belief, but also, this belief is supported by the fact that you did not even take the time to spell out the number three in the cover letter. In order to get a new job, you must not only avoid these errors at the onset, but throughout your employment.

During the employer's analysis of your cover letter and résumé, your grammar and punctuation must be impeccable.

- The more professional the position for which you apply, the narrower the margins should be. Candidates for legal positions should set their margins at three-quarters of an inch instead of 1 inch to create a more professional appearance.

- Be sure to use American spellings instead of British. For example, use the American spelling "judgment" instead of the British spelling "judgement."

- Résumés should contain parallel structures and consistent formatting between headings and lists of job responsibilities. For each job responsibility, you should use parallel structure in that nouns, power action verbs, and modifiers are in the same location for each bulleted item.

- The appearance and graphics design of your résumé and cover letter are important aesthetic considerations. If done appropriately, candidates with little or no experience can show a potential employer through the quality of their cover letters and résumés that they are indeed well versed and proficient with word processing skills needed for the position.

- Because the legal profession tends to be conservative, your résumé and cover letter should contain conservative fonts such as Times New Roman (the quintessential classic legal font), New Century Schoolbook, Padua, and Bookman. The graphics design chosen for your cover letter and letterhead, as well as résumé, may be served by using different fonts in a consistent pattern or format.

- Take time and care to develop a letterhead with your personal address for your correspondence with prospective employers. This adds a polished and professional touch.

- The use of graphic lines vertically and horizontally will ensure that different areas of your résumé stand out, but they are not necessarily required. There are many resources for drafting effective résumés and cover letters. You should review them with *the conservative nature of the legal profession* in mind.

OBJECTIVE STATEMENTS IN GENERAL

Objective statements are generally addressed in cover letters and need not necessarily be used in a résumé, unless effectively used to summarize the cover letter in one sentence. Before drafting a cover letter, you should draft an objective statement that will summarize the content of your cover letter in one sentence. Many applicants draft inappropriate objective statements that do not reiterate the content of their cover letters. These candidates generally draft poor cover letters as well. In a cover letter, you should state how your past activities show that you can fulfill position requirements and that you are professionally enthusiastic about discussing the position further. Cover letters and résumés are a prospective employer's first impression of you; make the presentation a powerful one.

When your résumé objective states, "I would like employment with a stable and reputable firm," the prospective employer begins to formulate opinions about you. With this objective, you could be perceived as self-interested. Perhaps you feel you are stable and reputable so you seek the same in an employer. You did not convey this. The objective statement should not be drafted in such a way that you appear self-absorbed and only interested in what an employer can offer you. The objective statement should succinctly state *what you want in a position and why you are entitled to it*, as explained in more detail in your cover letter.

This objective statement may also indicate your failure to investigate the firm or organization. It must fit the firm or organizational profile and state what you have to offer. If the employer is a brand new firm in its infancy, there may be much growth opportunity, but the stability and reputation may be uncertain. You may be perceived as unwilling to help develop the firm, since the objective statement indicates the foremost consideration—the desire for an established employer. Such an employer could perceive that you really want a big firm environment. You would probably not receive an interview in this case, since your objective does not fit the firm or organizational profile, and obviously you did not investigate the employer.

Some employers advertise for positions through bar journals and newspapers that contain blind post office box addresses. In these cases, you cannot adequately investigate the employer to tailor your submissions, and you will have limited knowledge of the skills and responsibilities required. If you tailor your experiences to what you know about the position requirements, however, you will not exclude yourself from consideration.

Objective statements should not personalize the potential employer, but focus on the position and firm opportunities. If the type of employer is critical to you, then you should apply only to those employers who meet your criteria. If you do so, then such an objective statement personalizing the employer will be unnecessary and, once again, your focus will be on the position.

OBJECTIVE STATEMENTS FOR ENTRY-LEVEL POSITIONS

An effective objective statement for an entry-level position might read, "Because I have a history of reliability and dedication, I seek a challenging and rewarding position with opportunity for increased responsibility as my expertise increases." This objective statement says much about what you have to offer and explains the type of position you are seeking. An employer who reads this will believe that you can support a history of reliability and dedication and therefore, can offer the same to the employer. Also, the employer will know you want to meet challenges and reap rewards by successfully facing them. This objective statement also indicates that you are looking for a long-term position with promotional opportunities that come as your expertise develops. The first part of the objective statement indicates confidence in your most emphasized qualities of reliability and dedication; the end of the objective statement indicates that you are humble and willing to work to earn promotions. This type of statement may be effectively used by an applicant seeking only an entry-level position. If you have experience, focus on your one or two best abilities and why you are entitled to the position you seek. Remember to be honest about this because if you are not, you will be found out and your employer will feel cheated.

PAST EMPLOYMENT DETAILS

Legal professionals should provide employment details tailored to position requirements. Beginning with a base résumé of work history and duties, you should compare them with those posted for the position. Then you should consider whether you had the same or similar duties in any past positions. If so, you will be in good shape. If not, you should rethink the scope of responsibilities with prior employers and see if there is some overlap of responsibilities. Ask yourself what problems you faced with prior employers and how you overcame those problems. You may also consider what accomplishments you had and how you managed them. The answers to these questions will likely demonstrate personal characteristics required for positions described in prior chapters in this book. Effective communications skills may be shown through any previous experiences, as can the ability to multitask. If you had no law-related experience, you should concentrate and focus your résumé content on how you exhibited the personal characteristics generally required for the position you are seeking.

ARRANGING THE RÉSUMÉ

When drafting a résumé, you should view it as the script you would like the interviewer to follow. Bite-sized tidbits of work-related accomplishments are generally preferred. You should arrange the content of your résumé chronologically, if you have relevant experience, or in order of priority, if you have little or no direct experience. How you choose to arrange your résumé will depend a great deal on the amount of education and experience you have had. For example, if you have had no education beyond high school, you may want to exclude such a reference in your résumé. If you have no job experience, but a wide range of extracurricular activities and experience, you may want to highlight your accomplishments in those activities.

CYBER RÉSUMÉS

Cyber résumés generally contain no formatting. Usually, Fortune 1000 companies have computerized applicant tracking systems that require résumés to have little or no formatting. This means that even if you use the United States Postal Service to deliver your résumé in lieu of the Internet, your résumé will still have to be scannable without formatting. The conservative formatting of legal résumés, exclusive of any graphic design lines, is highly likely to be scannable; more creative graphics design efforts will not be.

Cyber résumés and résumés scanned into computerized applicant tracking systems must contain the appropriate keywords that an employer selects based on a job description in order for the candidates to be selected as a potential interviewee. Without enough buzz words in a résumé, the computerized tracking system will not select it for consideration.

Aspiring legal professionals should demonstrate their legal skills through their past academic history, work experience, extracurricular activities, hobbies, and personal lives. By learning what legal skills are and demonstrating them in résumés and interviews, legal professionals can avoid employment rejection.

INTERVIEW EFFECTIVELY

You should develop your interview skills by going on as many interviews as possible. This will provide valuable interview experience through exposure to a variety of interview styles and techniques. Many employers first and foremost conduct a brief telephone interview to determine whether you possess the necessary qualifications and attitude to warrant an interview. During the initial telephone call, you may simply speak with an assistant to schedule an interview, or you may speak with the interviewer about the position available and whether your qualifications match. In either scenario, you should exhibit enthusiasm for the position and respond appropriately to questions and statements made.

THE SCREENING INTERVIEW

Organizations conduct on the average of one to three interviews with each prospective employee before making a final determination of who they will hire. Many types of interviews are conducted by different organizations, regardless of whether they have only one interview or a two- or three-tier stage of interviews. Usually, if there is a stage of interviews, the first interview will be with one or two people and is referred to as a *screening interview*. A screening interview is simply an opportunity to meet and determine if the candidate has the appropriate qualifications, enthusiasm, and look. The candidates who pass this screening interview advance to a *group interview* with a group of attorneys and administrative people.

THE GROUP/STRESS INTERVIEW

Group interviews may be conducted informally, where each group member can ask candidates questions regarding whatever they like, or they may be conducted more formally where each group member is assigned a particular line of inquiry. Group interviews can be called stress interviews—by the very nature of them, many candidates experience stress in them. They usually involve a candidate being seated at the end of a table separate from the group. The fact that the candidate must perform effectively before a group is stressful alone, even if there is a relatively simple line of inquiry. This stress factor may increase, depending on whether the attorneys barrage candidates with difficult questions or even contradict candidates to assess their stress reaction. Stress interviews are often conducted in stressful occupations. Because the legal field in general is so stressful, it is most likely that candidates will be exposed to stress interviews more than in any other profession without a college degree.

You should be aware that you may be subjected to a stress interview, and you should be prepared. You should investigate each employer before you interview so that you can exhibit some knowledge about the firm or organization. You will definitely be asked your knowledge about the firm or organization and questioned in depth about the skills you claimed on your résumé. For example, if your résumé states that you have assisted with all aspects of discovery, stress interviewers may ask a series of difficult questions in order to confirm the depth of your knowledge and experience. This may involve questions about state discovery laws. If you really had experience only drafting letters transmitting discovery documents and typing answers to interrogatories, you will appear to have misstated your experience on your résumé. Therefore, your experience information on a résumé should be precise, but brief. *Do not state that experience is extensive unless it truly is.* Take care to ensure that you do not embellish upon your experiences, because if you do, you will be found out.

ASKING QUESTIONS AT THE INTERVIEW

Make relevant and tactful inquiries at your interview. A candidate who is a sensitive listener will be able to gauge what types of questions are likely to be well received. Generally, you should formulate questions about the position, the firm or organization, the firm environment or atmosphere, and closing questions. First and foremost, you should show interest in the position and the people with whom you would work. This interest does not involve your salary or benefits. Do *not* ask questions about salary and benefits, unless the interviewer brings up the subject or has made an offer.

Make sure you have your questions answered about the firm or organization. Generally, you will not have to ask much, since many interviewers tell candidates about the firm or organization and position before they begin to question them. Employers do this for several reasons: One, to build rapport and place a candidate at ease prior to questioning, and, two, to let a candidate know what they want in an employee so that answers may be appropriately tailored. You should very carefully assess what is said to you in an interview and heed any cues you receive.

Questions about a firm's organization or atmosphere should never be asked directly; to do so, may demonstrate a lack of tact and even if the questions are asked directly, most interviewers sugarcoat their firm's philosophies and practices. The firm's atmosphere is probably your most important consideration, but no one in an interview is likely to say what the firm is really like— even if they did, perceptions may differ. This is why candidates should focus questions on the position available and ask fellow legal professionals about the firm instead of asking the interviewer.

Subtle questions in the context of position questions will give you clues about the firm's atmosphere. For example, instead of asking, "How high is your turnover?" You could more subtly ask about the person who previously occupied the position. After general questions about what that person's responsibilities were, you could ask, "Are there any additional responsibilities I would have" and "How long did [he or she] occupy that position?" The answer to the first question could indicate that the additional responsibilities are ones the previous employee did not have or that substantial job restructuring has occurred. The answer to the second question will give you some indication of turnover rate, without being so tactless as to directly ask. You can keep your questions focused on the position only as long as you do not ask too many questions about the prior employee. If you ask too many questions about the prior employee, your questioning purpose to concentrate on the position will be undermined. Upon reflection, the interviewer should remember how interested you were in the job instead of the previous employee.

Hopefully, during the interview process most questions will be answered. If not, you should ask all unanswered questions about the position and close with questions and statements that show the interviewer you want the job, if that is the case. In closing, you should exhibit enthusiasm and optimism about the position along with your ability to perform the job skills required.

- You should exude confidence, but still engage in a comfortable conversational style with the interviewer.

- You should be prepared with answers to questions about your personality, motivation or work ethic, education, experience, skills, career goals, and why you want the position. For example, instead of saying, "I am willing to work hard and have a strong work ethic," you would be better off saying, "I have always had a strong work ethic. With my last employer, I worked 60 hours a week and consistently met deadlines."

- You should not let an interview rattle you, even if it is a difficult one. If an interview causes a candidate discomfort, the job is probably not the right one.

Also, keep the following in mind.
1. Some interviews will be quite informal, in fact, the interviewer may simply want to speak and feel understood. Such an interviewer evaluates candidates' "auras" to see if they are compatible. The "aura test" is used especially when hiring young legal professionals who have rel-

atively little experience and whom the attorney plans to train, or by inexperienced interviewers.

2. Network and develop contacts in the legal community. Even if this networking does not lead to employment, you will develop contacts to provide you with insight into a firm. Because the legal profession is so adversarial, it is likely that if you look long and hard enough, you will find some negative feedback. However, some firms have such high turnover rates and bad reputations, that a candidate will be best served by finding this out before accepting an offer of employment instead of when it is too late. Also, candidates who do this before an interview will know whether to anticipate a stress interview and will develop more pertinent questions.

3. If an interviewer asks a startling question that causes your mind to go blank, ask him or her to please repeat the question. After it has been repeated, you should formulate your answer and give it. If you cannot, simply say you do not know. You should avoid blurting out wrong answers or any that could cause embarrassment in the future—if you are that anxious and nervous, the position with that organization is probably not for you at this point in your career or life anyway.

4. Candidates are almost always asked why they left prior employers or why they are looking for alternative employment. Be as honest and truthful as possible, in the most politically correct terms you can find. Focus on what you learned through the experience and do not speak negatively about prior employers or staff members.

Additional information about interviewing may be obtained from these web sites.

Job-Interview.net	http://www.job-interview.net
Career City Interview Tips	http://www.careercity.com/content/interview/index.asp
Interview Network	http://www.pse-net.com/interview/interview.htm
Interviewing Tips Link	http://www.jumpstartyourjobsearch.com
Kaplan's Hot Seat	http://kaplan.com/career/hotseat

Appendices

GLOSSARY OF TERMS*

Abstract of title: A chronological summary of all official records and recorded documents affecting the title to real property.

Action: Lawsuit before a court of justice; similarly referred to as cause of action or the facts in support of an action.

Alternative Dispute Resolution: Settlement of a dispute with assistance through mediation, conciliation, arbitration, and others, but without trial.

Answer: Defendant's item-by-item, paragraph-by-paragraph response to a petition or complaint.

Appeal: Resort to a superior court to review the decision of an inferior court or administrative agency; complaint to a higher tribunal of an error or injustice committed by a lower tribunal, in which the error or the injustice is sought to be corrected or reversed.

Arbitration: Form of alternative dispute resolution most similar to a trial, but held before an agreed-upon neutral third party who is not a judge with generally more relaxed and expedited procedures.

Bail bond: Money or other security provided to the court to temporarily allow a person's release from jail, assure their appearance in court, and compel that person to remain within the jurisdiction of the court (bail). An obligation signed by the accused to secure his or her presence at the trial. This obligation means that the accused may lose money by not properly appearing for the trial; often referred to simply as "bond." "Bail" and "bond" are often used interchangeably.

Bailiff: Court attendant who may also perform secretarial functions and who keeps order in the courtroom and is in charge of the jury.

Bankrupt: State or condition of being unable to pay one's debts as they are, or become, due.

Brief: Written statement that explains to a court relevant facts and applicable law and suggested resolution or relief desired.

Campaign: All the necessary legal and factual acts performed by a candidate and adherents to obtain a majority or plurality of the votes to be cast.

Case law: Aggregate of reported cases forming a body of jurisprudence, or the law of a particular subject as evidenced or formed by the judged cases, as distinguished from statutes and other sources of law.

Civil procedure: Rules and process that govern all procedural requirements of an action and appeal. These procedures address appellate procedures, pretrial and trial procedures, and the rules of evidence.

* Definitions adapted from *Black's Law Dictionary*: Centennial Edition (1891–1991), 6th edition.

Complaint: See petition.

Continuance: Postponement of a legal proceeding to a later date, or a request for lengthening the time.

Court reporter: Person who transcribes by shorthand or electronically records testimony during court proceedings or at trial-related proceedings such as depositions.

Cross-examination: Examination of a witness at a trial or a hearing, or when taking a deposition, by the opposing party, upon evidence given in chief, to test its truth, to further develop it, or for other purposes.

Deed: Conveyance of realty; a writing signed by the grantor, whereby the title to the realty is transferred from one to another.

Deposition: Oral statement made under oath before a court reporter regarding the subject matter of a lawsuit. Depositions may also be videotaped for later use at trial.

Direct examination: First interrogation or examination of a witness on the merits by the party on whose behalf the witness is called.

Discovery: In a general sense, the ascertainment of what was previously unknown; the disclosure or coming to light of what was previously hidden; the acquisition of notice of knowledge of given acts or facts, as, in regard to the discovery of fraud affecting the running of the statue of limitation, or the granting of a new trial for newly discovered evidence.

Docket: Calendar of any proceeding in a court of law; may also refer to the calendaring and scheduling process of a law office or other organization.

Elder Law: Practice of law involving specialized issue for legal services to the elderly and disabled, such as guardianship/capacity, health care, taxes, trusts and estates.

Ethics: Of or relating to moral action, conduct, motive, or character, as, ethical emotion; also, treating of moral feelings, duties, or conduct; containing precepts of morality; moral.

Evidence: Any proof, or probative matter, legally presented at a trial, by the act of the parties and through witnesses, records, documents, exhibits, or concrete objects.

Exhibit: Paper or document produced and exhibited to the court during a trial or hearing, or to a person taking depositions, or to auditors, arbitrators, etc.

Interrogatories: Set or series of written questions drawn up for the purpose of being propounded to a party, witness, or other persons having information of interest in the case.

Jury trial: Trial of matter or cause before a jury, as opposed to a trial before a judge.

Law: Rules laid down, ordained, or established; a rule or method according to which phenoms of actions coexist or follow each other. Law, in its generic sense, is a body of rules of action or conduct prescribed by controlling authorities.

Mediator: Neutral third person who helps disputing parties reach agreement through a process that helps parties agree to their own terms of settlement.

Motion to dismiss: Motion requesting that a complaint be dismissed because it does not state a claim for which the law provides a remedy, or is in some other way legally insufficient.

Order: Mandate, precept, command, or direction authoritatively given; rule or regulation.

PAC: Political Action Committiee. Group formed to receive contributions for use in an election campaign.

Personal liability: Kind of responsibility for the payment or performance of an obligation that exposes the personal assets of the responsible person to payment of the obligation.

Persuasion: Act of persuading; the act of influencing the mind by arguments or reasons offered, or by anything that moves the mind or passions, or inclines the will to determination.

Pleadings: Formal allegation by the parties to a lawsuit of their respective claims and defenses, with the intended purpose of providing notice about what is to be expected at trial.

Policy of insurance: Instrument in writing by which one party (insurer), in consideration of a premium, engages to indemnify another (insured) against a contingent loss, but making the insured a payment plan in compensation whenever the event shall happen by which the loss is to accrue.

Pretrial conference: Procedural device used prior to trial to narrow issues to be tried, to secure stipulations as to matters and evidence to be heard, and to take all other steps necessary to aid in the disposition of the case.

Quash: Motion to quash generally refers to a brief requesting that a court vacate or void a summons, subpoena, or other discovery request.

Separation agreement: Written agreement concerning custody, child support, alimony, and property division made by a married couple who are usually about to get a divorce or legal separation.

Service: Delivery of a legal document notifying a person or entity of a legal action; constitutes formal legal notice by an authorized person under state laws.

Statute: Formal written enactment of a legislative body, whether federal, state, city, or county; an act of legislature declaring, commanding, or prohibiting something; a particular law enacted and established by the will of the legislative department of the government; the written will of the legislature, solemnly expressed according to the forms necessary to constitute it the law of the state.

Statute of limitations: Time within which an initiating party must commence a lawsuit or lose the related causes of action.

Subpoena: Court order or other document requiring that certain documents or other items be produced, or compelling a witness to appear and testify.

Summary judgment: Court decision made on the basis of statements and evidence presented for the record without a trial, generally in the form of a brief with all attachments of statements and evidence; requested when a party believes there is no dispute about the facts of the case, and one party is entitled to judgment as a matter of law.

Trade secret: Plan or process, tool, mechanism, or compound known only to its owner and those employees in whom it is necessary to confide.

Transcript: Written word-for-word record of what was said prepared by a court reporter, either at a deposition or other court hearing or trial.

Trust: Legal entity created by a grantor for the benefit of designated beneficiaries under the laws of the state and the valid trust instrument.

Witness: In general, one who, being present, personally sees or perceives a thing or event; a beholder or spectator; one who is called to testify before a court.

Workers' Compensation Act: State and federal statutes that provide for fixed awards to employees or their dependants in case of employment-related accidents and illnesses, dispensing with the need by the employee to bring legal action and prove negligence on the part of the employer.

These are merely informational lay definitions designed to give a base understanding of the terms. They do not purport to be precise legal definitions in your state.

BIBLIOGRAPHY

Chapter One—Career Expectations in Law
Bachman, Walt. *Law* vs. *Life: What Lawyers Are Afraid to Say About the Legal Profession*. Rhinebeck, New York: Four Directions Press, 1995.

Chapter Two—Develop Realistic Expectations
Criscito, Pat, C.P.R.W. *Résumés in Cyberspace*, 2nd edition. Hauppauge, New York: Barron's Educational Series, Inc., 2000.

Hollander, David Adam, Esq., and Rob Tallia. *The Best Law Schools*, 1998 edition. New York: Random House, Inc., 1997.

Law School Admission Council. *The Official Guide to U.S. Law Schools*, 2000 edition. New York: Time Books Random House, 1999.

Walker, Aimee L., *http://www.dataoptions.com/temp.html*

Chapter Three—Legal Secretary
ALA Management Summary of September 2000 ALA Benefits Survey

Bureau of Labor Statistics, U.S. Department of Labor, *Occupational Outlook Handbook*, 2000–2001 edition. Washington, D.C.: Superintendent of Documents, U.S. Government Printing Office, 2000.

NALS® . . . the association for legal professionals
http://www.nals.org
Legal Secretaries International Inc.
http://www.compassnet.com/legalsec
International Association of Administrative Professionals
http://www.iaap-hq.org

Chapter Four—Legal Assistant
ALA Management Summary of September 2000 ALA Benefits Survey
American Association for Paralegal Education (AAFPE)
http://www.aafpe.org
American Bar Association
http://www.abanet.org/legalassts

Bureau of Labor Statistics, U.S. Department of Labor, *Occupational Outlook Handbook*, 2000–2001 edition. Washington, D.C.: Superintendent of Documents, U.S. Government Printing Office, 2000.

Hussey, Katherine Sheehy and Rick Benzel. *Legal & Paralegal Services on Your Home-Based PC*: New York: Windcrest/ McGraw-Hill, 1994.

Jacobstein, J. Myron and Roy M. Mersky. *Fundamentals of Legal Research*, 5th edition. New York: The Foundation Press, Inc., 1994.

National Association of Legal Assistants, Inc.
http://www.nala.org
National Federation of Paralegals Association.
http://www.paralegals.org

National Paralegal Association
http://www.nationalparalegal.org/
Nemeth, Charles P. *Paralegal Internship Manual*, 2nd edition. Dallas: Pearson Publication
Company, 1996.

Chapter Five—Legal Administrator
Association of Legal Administrators
http://www.alanet.org
ALA Management Summary of September 2000 ALA Benefits Survey

Chapter Six—Legal Marketing Professional
Legal Marketing Association
http://www.legalmarketing.org/
ALA Management Summary of September 2000 ALA Benefits Survey

Chapter Seven—Political Consultant
American Association of Political Consultants
http://www.theaapc.org/
Congressional Quarterly, Inc. and Campaigns and Elections Magazine. *Political Campaign Training
Seminar.* Friday, October 1, 1999.
Congressional Quarterly, Inc. and Campaigns and Elections Magazine. *Public Affairs and Grassroots
Lobbying.* September 30, 1999.
International Association of Political Consultants
http://www.iapc.org/

Chapter Eight—Court Reporter
Bureau of Labor Statistics, U.S. Department of Labor, *Occupational Outlook Handbook*, 2000–2001
edition. Washington, D.C.: Superintendent of Documents, U.S. Government Printing Office, 2000.
National Court Reporters Association
http://www.verbatimreporters.com
Potts, Kathleen E. Maki, ed. *Job Hunter's Sourcebook*, 4th edition. Farmington Hills, Michigan:
The Gale Group, 1999.

Chapter Nine—Private Investigator
Bureau of Labor Statistics, U.S. Department of Labor, *Occupational Outlook Handbook*, 2000–2001
edition. Washington, D.C. Superintendent of Documents, U.S. Government Printing Office, 2000.
Fallis, Greg and Ruth Greenberg. *Be Your Own Detective*. New York: M. Evans and Company, Inc.,
1998.
National Association of Investigative Specialists, Inc.
http://www.pimall.com/nais/links.html
Potts, Kathleen E. Maki, ed. *Job Hunter's Sourcebook*, 4th edition. Farmington Hills, Michigan:
The Gale Group, 1999.
Thomas, Ralph. *How to Investigate by Computer*, 1999 edition. Austin, Texas: Thomas
Investigative Publications, Inc., 1999.
Tyska, Louis A. and Lawrence J. Fennelly. *Investigations—150 Things You Should Know.* Woburn,
Massachusetts: Butterworth-Heinemann Publications, 1999.

Chapter Ten—Deputy Court Clerk

Bureau of Labor Statistics, U.S. Department of Labor, *Career Guide to Industries*, 2000–2001 edition. Washington, D.C.: Superintendent of Documents, U.S. Government Printing Office, 2000.

Bureau of Labor Statistics, U.S. Department of Labor, *Occupational Outlook Handbook*, 2000–2001 edition. Washington, D.C.: Superintendent of Documents, U.S. Government Printing Office, 2000.

Court Clerk's Association Board of Directors. *Handbook for Court Clerks of Oklahoma*. Stillwater, Oklahoma: The Center for Local Government Technology, Oklahoma State University, 2000.

National Association for Court Management

http://www.nacmnet.org

National Center for State Courts

http://www.ncsc.dni.us/

National Conference of Appellate Court Clerks

http://www.ncsc.dni.us/ncacc/ncacc.html

Farr, Michael J. and LaVerne Ludden. *The O*Net Dictionary of Occupational Titles*, 1998 edition. Indianapolis: Jist Works, Inc., 1998.

Chapter Eleven—Mediator

Allen, Elizabeth L. and Donald D. Moore. *Affordable Justice: How to Handle any Dispute Out of Court*. California: Westcoast Press, 1997.

Fisher, Roger and William Ury. *Getting to Yes: Negotiating Without Giving In*, 2nd edition. Cambridge: Harvard University Project.

Supreme Court of Oklahoma. *State of Oklahoma Alternative Dispute Resolution System Mediation Training and Resource Manual*, 1997.

The American Academy of Mediators

http://www193.pair.com/afm/afmmedorg.html

Chapter Twelve—Legal Support Providers

Bureau of Labor Statistics, U.S. Department of Labor, *Career Guide to Industries*, 2000–2001 edition. Washington, D.C.: Superintendent of Documents, U.S. Government Printing Office, 2000.

Bureau of Labor Statistics, U.S. Department of Labor, *Occupational Outlook Handbook*, 2000–2001 edition. Washington, D.C.: Superintendent of Documents, U.S. Government Printing Office, 2000.

Criscito, Pat, C.P.R.W. *Résumés in Cyberspace*, 2nd edition. Hauppauge, New York: Barron's Educational Series, Inc., 2000.

Farr, Michael J. and LaVerne Ludden. *The O*Net Dictionary of Occupational Titles*, 1998 edition. Indianapolis: Jist Works, Inc., 1998.

Hussey, Katherine Sheehy and Rick Benzel. *Legal & Paralegal Services On Your Home-Based PC*. New York: Windcrest/McGraw-Hill, 1994.

Munneke, Gary. *Careers in Law*, 2nd edition. Lincolnwood (Chicago): VGM Career Horizons, 1997.

Chapter Thirteen—Find the Job That Is Right for You

Bachman, Walt. *Law* vs. *Life: What Lawyers Are Afraid to Say About the Legal Profession*. Rhinebeck, New York: Four Directions Press, 1995.

Chapter Fourteen—Get the Job You Want

Beatty, Richard H. *The Five-Minute Interview*, 2nd edtion. New York: John Wiley & Sons, Inc.

Criscito, Pat, C.P.R.W. *Designing the Perfect Résumé*, 2nd edition. Hauppauge, New York: Barron's Educational Series, Inc., 2000.

Criscito, Pat, C.P.R.W. *Résumés in Cyberspace*, 2nd edition. Hauppauge, New York: Barron's Educational Series, Inc., 2000.

Holder, Philip T. and Donna Lea Hawley. *The Executive Protection Professional's Manual*. Woburn, Massachusetts: Butterworth-Heinemann Publications, 1998.

Kennedy, Joyce Lain. *Résumés for Dummies*, 3rd edition. Foster City, California: IDG Books Worldwide, Inc., 2000.

Krannich, Caryl Rae, Ph.D. and Ronald L. Krannich, Ph.D. *101 Dynamite Answers to Interview Questions: Sell Your Strengths!* 4th edition. Manassas Park, Virginia: Impact Publications, 1999.

Noble, David F. *Professional Résumés for Accounting, Tax Finance, and Law*, 2000 edition. Indianapolis: Jist Publishing, 2000.

Pincus, Marilyn. *Interview Strategies That Lead to Job Offers: The Skills You Need to Succeed in the Business World*. Hauppauge, New York: Barron's Educational Series, Inc., 1999.

Wilson, Robert F. and Adele Lewis. *Better Résumés for Executives and Professionals*, 4th edition. Hauppauge, New York: Barron's Educational Series, Inc., 2000.

THE AUTHOR

Tracy A. Cinocca is licensed to practice law in Oklahoma; she operates her own general law practice, Tracy A. Cinocca, P.C. As an undergraduate at the University of Oklahoma, Ms. Cinocca promoted legislative reform for higher education and obtained her Bachelor of Arts degree. While employed in contract negotiation and product acquisition, Ms. Cinocca completed her masters in Business Administration from Oklahoma City University.

In the fall of 1997, Ms. Cinocca obtained her juris doctorate from the University of Tulsa College of Law with a health law certification (Phi Delta Phi legal fraternity). The following spring she was admitted to practice law in the State of Oklahoma, Northern, Eastern, and Western Districts. She is the author of "The Need for a Family Medical Decision-Making Statute in Oklahoma" published December 26, 1998 in the *Oklahoma Bar Journal*. Ms. Cinocca primarily practices in civil business litigation, personal injury, employment discrimination, and family law.

Index

A

Abstractors, 149–150
American:
    Academy of Family Mediators,
    The, 140
    Association:
        for Paralegal Education, 50
        of Political Consultants, 88
    Bar Association, 50
Association of Legal Administrators,
    60

B

Bail bondsmen, 145–146
Bailiffs, 143–144
Business litigation, 15

C

Career:
    choice, 153–161
    expectations, 1–7
    options, evaluating, 153–156
    planning, 18–20
Civil litigation, 15
Code of conduct, 6
Communications law, 15
Competition, 6–7
Council of Better Business Bureaus,
The, 140
Court reporter, 91–99
    case example, 95–97
    duties, 92–93
    earnings, 98
    employment forecast, 98
    getting started, 97–98
    professional organizations,
    99
    skills, 91–92
    work routine, 93–94
Cover letters, 165
    objective statements, 167
Criminal law, 16
Curriculum courses, 9–10

D

Debate classes, 10
Depositions, 42
Deputy Court Clerk, 117–125
    case example, 120–122
    duties, 118–119
    earnings, 123
    employment forecast, 123
    getting started, 122

    professional organizations,
    123–124
    records, 119
    skills, 117–118
    work routine, 119
Discovery, 41–42
Documents, preparation, 40–41
Drama classes, 11

E

Educational preparation, 9–11
Employers, potential, 154–155
Employment:
    offers, evaluating, 159–160
    prior, 14–16
Environment, 5
Environmental law, 16
Ethics, 6
Examiners, 149–150
Exhibits, 42
Expectations, 1–7
    developing realistic, 9–21
Extracurricular activities, 11

F

Facts, checking, 3–5
File clerks, 148–149
Fund-raising, 80–81

G

General law, 15

H

Health care law, 14

I

Insurance:
    claims:
        adjusters, 144–145
        clerks, 144–145
    defense, 14
Intellectual property, 16
International:
    Association of:
        Administrative Professionals,
        33
        Political Consultants, 88
    law, 16
Internet resources, 12–14, 104–105,
139, 147
    career sites, 157–158, 173
Internships, 11–12
Interpreters, 149
Interviews, 169–173

group, 170
questions, 171–173
screening, 169–170
stress, 170

L

Law:
    librarians, 146–147
    office skills, 15–16
Legal:
    administrator, 53–61
        case example, 57–58
        duties, 54–55
        earnings, 59–60
        employment forecast, 59
        getting started, 59
        professional organizations,
        60
        skills, 54
        work routine, 55–56
    analysis, 3
    assistant, 37–51
        brief writing, 47
        case example, 44–46
        duties, 39–43
        earnings, 49
        employment forecast,
        48–49
        getting started, 46–47
        internships, 47–48
        Management Association,
        50
        professional organizations,
        50–51
        skills, 38–39
        time management, 48
        work routine, 43
    experience, benefits, 150–151
    marketing professional, 63–75
        case example, 68–72
        duties, 64–66
        earnings, 73
        employment forecast,
        72–73
        professional organization,
        74
        skills, 63–64
        work routine, 66–67
    Marketing Association, 74
    Secretaries International, 33
    secretary, 23–35
        case example, 28–30
        duties, 25–27
        earnings, 33